"*Rivers are mirrors. We pursue trout and find an elusive something in ourselves.*"

-Cathy Newman, National Geographic April 1996

TRIBUTARIES

Fly-fishing Sojourns to the Less Traveled Streams

Lou Wentz

Dedicated to the memory of Jack Steel, who told me many great stories, none about fly-fishing.

Special Thanks

To Carol, Willow and Daisy, who endured my intermittent absence to pursue my fly-fishing passion.

Coast Fork Press

Eugene, Oregon

Book Marketing Services
Coast Fork Press

P.O. 40991
Eugene, OR 97404
www.coastforkpress.com

Editorial Services
Hayden Seder
P.O. Box 3896 | Ketchum, ID| 83340
www.haydenseder.com

Cover Art
Pen and ink drawing
Bob Myrick
Easton, PA

Print ISBN 978-1-09838-626-9

eBook ISBN 978-1-09838-627-6

CONTENTS

INTRODUCTION

In June of 2019, while sitting in my room at the Oasis Café and Motel in Juntura, Oregon, I'm contemplating a decades long fly-fishing journey that led me to this place in that moment of time. The quarters contain four motel units, a restaurant, a few RV slips, and a couple of "permanent" trailers. I doubt that more than 36 residents inhabit this unincorporated village in Malheur County. The stream I visit on this trip, the Malheur River, flows east through this arid, hauntingly beautiful landscape, eventually reaching the Snake River at Oregon's eastern border. It is surely a less traveled stream by all measures. I encountered nary another angler—nor any trout for that matter—in the three days I've encamped here. My guidebook may have been dated, but there are supposed to be trout in this river, mostly hatchery plants that survive harsh conditions. It is a place that few call a fishing destination, hence its appeal. I tend to choose fishing locations or times of year that will afford me a more solitary experience, but occasionally I incidentally appreciate encounters with strangers, some of whom fish, and others who might not have any connection to the sport. Aside from those encounters, I tend toward introspection when I fish. That's not to say

I am not serious about catching fish on every outing, but my success is not necessarily measured in pounds or inches. Though I am formulating this introduction in a far western corner of the United States, the streams from which this eclectic gathering of writings cover might be quite familiar to anglers of Pennsylvania or the Catskills. Here is the list, in no particular order: *Neshaminy Creek, Octoraro Creek, Penns Creek, Schoharie Creek, Beaverkill, East Branch of the Delaware, West Branch of the Delaware, Manatawny Creek, Frankford Creek, Lackawanna River, Wissahickon Creek, Valley Creek, Bushkill Creek (Easton), Hosensack Creek, Perkiomen Creek,* and *Tulpehocken Creek.* All are tributaries to larger systems, and most have wild trout in them, though in some of those creeks trout may have arrived via the nearest two-lane county road.

Outside of a few selections, it seems most books on fly-fishing these days drill into technique, fly selection, and location in order to demonstrate how to catch more and bigger fish. I make no grandiose claims, but like any fly-fishing volume, the reader may infer a technique or hint that will enable better fishing. But that is not the purpose of this book. Rather, I would like to suggest that the book will allow the reader to catch more of what fishing offers outside the quest for handsome fish. It is the chance to immerse in the wider encounter that gives depth, texture, and emotion to the fishing experience. As to some of the topics and themes covered, many reach outside of the fishing culture and I would suggest that the non-angler can get just as much enjoyment out of this book as their angling counterparts. In full disclosure, the less traveled streams are a metaphor for events and circumstances that mark the experience as being memorable, unique, and in some cases self-reflective. For many this feature of fishing generally finds itself around campfires and long drives with companions to far-flung destinations. And as with many stories from a more distant past, memory and the facts often diverge but there are numerous strands of truth braided together in this book to make a plausible case for an honest telling. In self-defense, I do reserve the right to feign ignorance if confronted with a differing version of the same event.

As you may guess by thumbing through some of these pages, the chapters herein contain a memoir of forty years of fly-fishing, some while I was a novitiate, a few while I was proficient, and a scattering from the in-between stages during the many years I lived in Pennsylvania. I pay a few homages along the way, to Art Flick and John Burroughs in "Catskill Remembrances" and Richard Brautigan in "The Amish Boy." The topical subject of vegan philosophy versus catch-and-release can be sifted from "Siren of Shangri-La," while "Demons" offers a peek into inner psychology. "Natal Streams" explores the roots of a passion for fishing, wondering what role genes and culture each play. "Redeeming Currents" touches upon urban fishing along Bushkill Creek and my encounter with an underprivileged young boy from a disadvantaged neighborhood in Easton, Pennsylvania. "The New World" entails a coming-of-age fishing chronicle. In full confession, the opening dialogue (May 1969) is speculative as the only facts I could ascertain were that Indian Joe's part-time job was lost when a rope mill in Hulmeville, Pennsylvania closed, leading some to believe he could no longer pay taxes on his holding. I did hear that he moved on to the Pocono region of Pennsylvania. The rest of the events and dialogue are as true as I could remember them. I would be remiss if I did not disclose that in some of these tracts, the names have been changed to protect the innocent (and the guilty). "Tulpehocken Dreams" preserves some of my best days on the water as I graduated from neophyte to accomplished angler. Though most of my fishing is done alone, "Drought Fishing" celebrates fishing with friends as we commiserate over the bad luck of seasonal drought in less-than-elegant fashion. "Last Cast" evokes how meaningful the end of an outing, a trip, a season or even a lifetime of fishing might be experienced. "Woodward Cave" attempts to uncover personal enlightenment in literally the darkest of places. Of course, what fly-fishing volume could be considered complete without addressing the Zen of fly-fishing as I venture in "Wild Black Raspberries."

The birthing of this book began more than thirty years ago when I became deeply involved with my local Trout Unlimited Chapter, Perkiomen Valley (#332). After having acquired sufficient skill as an angler, it is not hard to make the obvious connection between fly-fishing and the habitat where trout live. Unfortunately, even though Trout Unlimited has roughly 350,000 members today and has been in existence since 1954, not much in the angling literature appears to affirm the blood, sweat, and tears that members of local chapters produce in their efforts to make watersheds more sustainable for the fish that most fly anglers purport to love. "Perkiomen Nightmares" aims to correct that deficiency in hopes that writers more gifted than I can pay forward the work of a great organization and the loyal, hard-working volunteers. There are very few among us who are not beneficiaries of TU stream and watershed enhancements that have taken place in our local and distant destinations in search of trout. To show my appreciation, a portion of the proceeds of each book sold online will be dedicated to the national organization.

Tight Lines,

Lou Wentz

Eugene, OR

1

The Amish Boy

The small, cramped bookstore spewed a cornucopia of literary abundance, the many shelves bowing under the weight of both celebrated and obscure authors and topics popular to arcane. I scanned the listings and made my way to the section that I wanted, having decided before entering the little shop in Center City Philadelphia that it was time for some refreshing reading to ward off the dulling effects of mandatory college courses. My wandering into that place on a warm May afternoon in 1969 on the commute home after classes at Temple seems predestined, looking back on it now. I remembered feeling pleased with finding myself in the poetry section. Poetry was a new art form for me back then. English was not my major, so poetry was a source of expression that was peculiar and distinctive, a kind of acquired taste that covertly frees the imprisoned spirit. I especially relished the irreverence of the Beat poets—Ferlinghetti and Corso in particular. They defied traditions in social mores and writing style of their era and pushed the boundaries beyond the chain-link fence of conventional literature. On that particular day, my mind was begging for a new challenge.

As a boy my favorite books were about the outdoors— Jack London stories, anything about explorers in the West and Great North Woods, and—oh yes— fishing stories. My uncle's hand-me-down copies of *Field and Stream* and *Outdoor Life* were prized possessions that were stashed under my bed for nighttime reading with a flashlight when I was supposed to be sleeping. Trout fishing in far-off, adventurous places held my fascination and took me to regions far beyond my own experiences growing up in a family of limited means on the populous east coast. I had a yearning for distant places, literally and figuratively. And in a roundabout way, my thirst for new places eventually ushered me to the poetry section of that bookstore.

I rapidly scanned the titles for something that would catch my fancy when my eyes seized upon a captivating title. There was a thin paperback book that seemed out of place—perhaps wrongly filed by a careless clerk—that caught my attention. I turned my head sideways and studied the narrow edge to confirm what I thought I saw at first glance. *TROUT FISHING IN AMERICA* jumped out at me like a cheap bottle of beer in a mineral water display. I fingered the top corner of the book and tipped it toward me. On inspecting the cover, I puzzled over the two hippies, a man and a woman, dressed in the retro garb stylish at that time known as "digger" clothing, a style made popular by San Francisco street theater actors who rummaged through thrift shops to assemble a functional and fashionable hip wardrobe that was the inexpensive alternative to more traditional, conforming styles popularized by the major media. The man was Richard Brautigan. The woman, I assumed, was his wife or girlfriend. When I examined the table of contents, I realized that the book was a crazy, witty, fantasy excursion by a wonderfully demented mind. I started thumbing through the pages, scanning paragraphs occasionally the way you do before deciding to buy, to get a feel for the content and the writing. I quickly began to admire the work of an original trout bum. References to characters like Trout Fishing in America Shorty and a chapter titled "A Walden Pond for Winos" caused me to grin conspicuously. This was very original writing, with a loose theme of trout fishing in America as a vehicle holding it together. My appetite whetted, I had to have it. I made my way over to the counter and plunked two ones down to cover the $1.95 printed on the jacket. Unknowingly at the time, I walked out of that store with the first book of my fly-fishing library. Reading through it in one day, underlining phrases and paragraphs as if I were assigned an explication by an English prof, I scrutinized the writing style and chuckled at the bizarre and sometimes fantastic images portrayed in this group of whimsical songs, stories, and poems. Brautigan immortalized the phrase TROUT FISHING IN AMERICA, tendering an inverted metaphor of wholesome, fundamental values as integral as truth and justice, which he twists and distorts with each absurd tale. At times he used the title as a pseudonym when he makes first-person references. In other instances, it's a personification for poets and street urchins (which I supposed were one and the same to him). It's a strange and wonderful tour through a mind that challenged borders, which saw the American experience through a kaleidoscope instead of lenses. A celebration of creativity, his writing inspires whimsy and fantasy, irreverence, and defiance, with splashes of magic and mimicry. I still have the original copy and keep it where it appropriately belongs, among my fishing titles.

Underneath his eccentric demeanor, Richard Brautigan was a troubled individual who overcame harsh circumstances growing up in a dysfunctional, working-class family in Eugene, Oregon. His most prolific years were spent in the Bay Area dancing among the icons of the counterculture of the late 1960s. Sadly, he committed suicide in a remote cabin in Northern California in 1984. He was eulogized in one of the national fly-fishing magazines, and Russell Chatham mourned his friend in *Dark Waters*. I prefer to remember him through the daft and splendid essays in *TROUT FISHING IN AMERICA*.

*   *   *   *   *   *   *   *

The Octoraro Creek winds through southeastern Pennsylvania, forming the border of Chester and Lancaster Counties for some thirty miles. It is largely farm country, though signs of encroaching development spring up on formerly tilled fields, planned communities plopped incongruously among the dairy herds, alfalfa fields, and Amish farmsteads. The creek itself presents that odd mix of healthy riparian buffer and bare, eroded banks from neglectful agricultural practices. At one point it meanders through a state gamelands long enough to be cooled by the shading of mature oaks and maples. There the stream is about twenty to thirty feet wide with a series of modestly deep pools spaced by gentle riffles. Though Lancaster County has among the highest number of limestone-influenced streams in Pennsylvania, they are almost all warmed and silted due to extensive overgrazing. The Octararo is one of the few streams in the area capable of holding trout for a delayed-harvest fly-fishing experience. Past the special regulations zone, about seven or so miles, the stream empties into a reservoir. After it leaves the reservoir, as it flows toward the Maryland border, it takes a serpentine course through a unique geological formation that contains rare and endangered species of plant life unlike anything in the surrounding area. The Nature Conservancy bought a huge tract in this area to preserve its original character. On a mild, windless day in May many years ago, I made this my ultimate destination, that is, after a stop at the project waters. Accounts from historical papers suggested that shad made it up this stream at one time, which empties into the Susquehanna a few miles on the other side of the Maryland border. Nobody ever talked up or wrote about this stream, so I figured that there might be some discoveries to be made. Perhaps a stray shad or a spawning smallmouth? Safe to say, a less traveled stream that offered a welcome respite from the rigors of trout madness.

When I pulled into the parking area by the state gamelands, I noticed the trees had finally filled out to a fresh, leafy fullness that was typical of late May. Determined to scout out this place, I hopped out of my van to get a better look at my surroundings. The shaded woodland released a fragrance of damp, fertile soil mixed with the decaying leaves from last year's fall. My feet sunk slowly with each step on the spongy mat as I made my way over to the bridge, something anglers always do to size up a new stream. *Should I fish upstream or down?* A glance upstream gave me the answer. A fisherman was crouched by the edge of a small pool, trying to delicately place his fly in the current next to a fallen log that offered some sanctuary for an enterprising trout. I like to fish alone, and I don't particularly like to disturb others if I can help it, so downstream was where I would be headed.

My rod already strung in the back of the van, I lifted it out for its baptism into these marginal waters. After I slid into my waders and donned my vest, I crept to the edge of the stream. Tying on a caddis emerger, I drifted it downstream through promising holes. After a few casts, the familiar tug of surprised resistance signaled up the line. A nice twelve-inch rainbow fought his way to my outreached hand. I slipped the rubbery fish off the hook and slogged downstream about fifty yards. In the next shallow riffle, I encountered a retreating angler with an aura of defeat written on his face, revealed by his downcast eyes and tired glance. I ask about his luck anyway, and he tells me of a pod of fish at the head of the next pool sipping tiny flies. He says no more, but by inference he revealed that he didn't take them. Special project waters like this can be heavily fished, so these fish were probably wise by now.

It happens even to those lowly hatchery fish that most anglers despise in theory but who have trouble with them once they've been to school. What the hell, I thought, it's still trout fishing.

I reached the head of the pool and sure enough, four or five dainty rises appear at regular intervals. My gaze fixed on the chalky water, but I saw nothing that resembled a hatch. I glanced at the rays of sunlight piercing the few holes the trees refused to cover. Sometimes you can spot a newly hatched fly in these telltale openings, looking almost like a tiny-winged fairy rather than the real thing. After a minute or so, I saw what looks to be a blue-winged olive dancing in the sunlit space above the cool flow of the stream. I tie on a #18 BWO floating nymph and cast to the closest rise form. A pinch that pops out. Problem solved. Right fly. I take four browns in the next twenty minutes and sting a few others. I've had enough though. I came for the untested waters downstream another twenty miles, so I swaggered confidently in my chest waders back to the van.

I drove through the part of Lancaster County considered the heart of Amish country. These peculiar people settled here on William Penn's promise of religious freedom back in the colonial days. Two hundred and fifty-some years later, while the rest of the world was spinning out of control toward the twenty-first century, these people have spurned modern developments like the automobile and electricity as part of their religious covenant. They're conscientious objectors and live a life of what is known today as voluntary simplicity. Often referred to as the "plain people" for their customs and dress, they generally shy away from involvement in larger society, preferring to socialize among their own close-knit communities. To say that these people are conservative—in the true meaning of the word—is an understatement.

In the late 1960s, the state of Pennsylvania tried to force a closing of the Amish schools, claiming that most of the youngsters dropped out by the age of fourteen to work on family farms, which was essentially true. It was one of the few times this community, which usually unites for barn raisings, rallied to defend their culture. The strongest arguments they and their advocates offered were quite compelling. In a larger society where crime and divorce rates were soaring out of control, theirs were virtually nonexistent. The kind of citizens that the public school system hoped to create in the most utopian of scenarios were quietly being produced in little one-room schoolhouses heated with potbellied stoves. They live as a tight community, in harmony with nature, practicing low-impact farming methods and lifestyles, respecting their neighbors, and valuing the family. Hell, if the state had public interest in mind, they'd force everybody to go to Amish schools. Eventually, the wisdom of their simplicity prevailed, and the state backed down and the field of education took a reluctant step forward.

I made my way on gravel backroads, peering intently out my dusty windshield. The bright sun penetrated the sharp blue sky, blessing the fields and pastures below. Sunday, being the Lord's Day, meant that the hard-working Amish had a day off, which they generally spent visiting others in the sect—after services of course. I passed a few horse-drawn carriages on those farm lanes, their outmoded conveyances crowded with young families toting small children and others transporting wizened elders. I turned on to a much-improved macadam road headed toward my destination, appreciating the scenery as I sped along. The anticipation of this new place swelled within me as I tried to imagine its features from the serpentine contours splayed across the creased folds of the map spread out on my passenger seat. I tried to visualize it in relation to previous jaunts to similar places, though I've yet to come across a place that matched my imaginary expectations. It seems that every stream defines its own character, no matter how lowly or neglected.

As I approached a gentle incline ahead, my attention was drawn to a slight figure on the opposite side of the road: a small Amish boy was headed in my direction, dressed in traditional black coat and pants, blue shirt, and straw hat. Something was unusual about his gait, a kind of rhythmic wobbling that seemed out of character, so I slowed down to get a better look. As I approached, I gazed in utter amazement. It was an Amish boy on Rollerblade skates, the kind of equipment you'd expect to see from spunky teenagers gliding on the boardwalk down at the shore. Skating blithely down the incline, carrying a small package, his rhythmic bounce defied my conception of the stoic Amish. When I passed him, I broke out into a huge grin. He smiled back and we simultaneously waved to each other. A rush of emotion came over me that hastened to elation. Trout Fishing in America Shorty lives! The Amish boy is TROUT FISHING IN AMERICA!

2

Natal Streams

"Now this was the way in which the boy came in to possession of his undreaded rod. He was by nature and heredity one of those predestined anglers whom Izaak Walton tersely describes as 'born so.' His earliest passion was fishing."

-Henry Van Dyke, *Little Rivers*

I recently made a temporary move back to Pennsylvania after a seven-year stint in Oregon, for reasons too complicated to discuss here. By necessity, I had to acquire new health insurance and get assigned to a family physician in the Pocono region of Pennsylvania. On my first visit to the doctor—more of a meet-and-greet and review of my medical status than any treatment—we got to talking about our pasts. It turns out we were both born at Frankford Hospital, though he at the annex in Langhorne in Bucks County, and I in the original hospital in the gritty, blue collar Frankford neighborhood of Philadelphia. We discussed the metrics sociologists use to forecast outcomes based on current statistics and concluded that there was a better chance of finding a chess champion than a fly angler in my old 19124 ZIP code. That neighborhood, the place where my father was born and raised, was white working-class when I was born. Picture dart bars with cheap beers on tap and patrons cursing at the Phils on the black-and-white TV perched on a corner stand on a Friday evening, where the pay checks get invested before groceries are bought. Inhaling fumes at Barrets Chemical bestowed a certain leniency to those who might judge. That was one of the better jobs, with compensation tied to the danger quotient. The plant is still there after a succession of owners, though the neighborhood has more skin complexions than just white these days. Most of the other mills and factories have shuttered and either moved south or just closed. The Frankford Creek would have been my natal stream. One of its tributaries, the Wingohocking Creek, has had much of its length converted to a storm sewer, getting channeled underground through round concrete pipes while streets were paved above it. Other tributaries suffered a similar fate. The Clean Water Act was not even imagined when all this occurred. Needless to say, I doubt I would have taken up fishing if I had to bike past raucous foundries, avoiding broken beer bottles and errant stray dogs to sling a line in a slime-filled lagoon. It's not the kind of nature one finds to immerse the soul for spiritual healing, let alone an edible meal.

According to my father, my grandfather (his dad) was a gifted saltwater angler, gifted in the sense that he was extremely adept at locating fish in the Barnegat Bay, the favored saltwater fishing location where catching and keeping were the order of the day. I never got to fish with my paternal grandfather. He died of a heart attack at age 47, when I was just a toddler. Smoking and a bad diet will do that to you. At the age of eight, my family moved from Frankford to the almost-middle-class district north of Philadelphia known as Bensalem Township. My father took me and my next older brother on yearly trips to the Barnegat Bay starting when I was nine until about the age of fourteen. He never had the knack of finding fish the way his dad could, though some trips brought bounty while others proved almost futile. Then the trips suddenly stopped. But not to worry, I had plenty of opportunity to explore the Neshaminy Creek, a mere 300 yards from our modest home.

*　　*　　*　　*　　*　　*　　*　　*

The Lackawanna River carves through the anthracite coal region in northeastern Pennsylvania, along the old mining towns of Carbondale, Archibald, Jermyn, Peckville, and Oliphant, before meeting the North Branch of the Susquehanna River in Scranton. The towns, connected one after the other without noticeable boundary, are almost entirely made up of two-story, aluminum-sided, working-class residences, all painted white at one time, but now sullied with the distinctive stain of benign neglect that conveys a lack of distinguishing character. There's a sense of muted desperation about the place that evokes a feeling of estrangement, that suggests morbid fear hides behind the tarnished entrance doors. While we were driving through there one time, my wife pronounced it as "what it's like to be in a place without art."

The river itself has made an amazing recovery from coal silt, mine acid, and industrial pollution to become a pretty fair trout stream, though when you go there you can still see the remnants of its derelict past. Culm piles and abandoned railroad lines parallel much of the stream. Although a two-and-a-half-hour drive away from my home waters, I went there one May for—on the surface—a fishing outing to an unfamiliar stream. The regulations booklet, as well as some favorable press, suggested that some large, wild trout inhabited those waters. Hindsight being 20/20, I think the purpose of the trip was retrospective. My mother grew up in Peckville among those dreary coal towns. She shared a lot of fond memories about being raised poor in a merged family of twelve brothers and sisters from thrice-married parents, marriages of economic convenience more than romantic interludes. But the toll of dirty coal work and hard times bears an unfair price to pay. Her father died of black lung disease when she was eleven, and the widow who couldn't afford a shoe, let alone live in one, moved the family downstate to Philadelphia when World War II broke out to take advantage of better opportunity. It's where my mother eventually met my father, and the rest, you might say, is more destiny.

I did get to find out what influence a place has on molding personality and character, a question that often surfaced whenever I thought about what possibilities may have unfolded for me—the me with a different father, dissimilar genes, and disparate culture—had my mother's family stayed in the coal region and she married otherwise. During a break from fishing the Lackawanna, after a pleasant midweek morning that yielded a sizable brookie and two browns— all wild, healthy fish—I decided to wander over to the local luncheonette for a quick bite before moving on to another section of the river. Though I was dressed a step down from causal, the waitress barely looked at me as she stated gruffly that I could sit wherever I wanted. I chose a booth in the front, by the door, and took the seat facing the rest of the dining room. At first, I thought she was reacting to my unkempt, unshaven fishing demeanor. In a few minutes, the place became more revealing. The fluorescent lighting in the dining room cast a dull luster on the Formica tabletops, busy with plate exchanges of hamburgers, goulash, and other bland comfort foods ordered by the local clientele. The place was three-quarters full on a Wednesday afternoon—regulars, I quickly surmised. Whenever I looked in the direction of another person, their eyes quickly averted, as if making eye contact would throw them severely off balance. Yet when I looked down toward the table at my menu, I could feel their eyes calculating instantly on my being. My fair skin and amiable expression contrasted starkly from their weathered, defeated demeanors. I felt instantly unwelcome, like some bearer of bad news from the front. This was more than the usual punctuated snubbing you get from intruding into rural haunts. Their piercing, unapproving glances stabbed me every time I peeked above the menu. Theirs was more of a silent resentment pervading sullen, drained eyes. For the first time, I viscerally understood Ralph Ellison's invisible man, discounted almost out of existence by the townsfolk I was encountering. Diminished on one level, yet I could feel an unspoken bitterness and fear residing in their estimation of my presence. It appeared obvious that the white working-class crowd, dreary of inane soap operas and losing lottery tickets, with no appetite for outsiders, had little appreciation for any revelations that might be offered by blue-jeaned messengers like me. It seemed as if my presence alone was forcing them to come face to face with their other selves which had no knowledge of the cultural and economic forces that turned their lives into narrow, dark passages. When mines close and work ends, days pass while opinions retreat to safe, familiar dungeons. It was an accidental discovery for me, but I will pass it on for what it is worth. Don't underestimate the latter in the nature versus nurture argument of what shapes us all. I could have been one of them.

*　　　*　　　*　　　*　　　*　　　*　　　*

Although it might not seem like it from a micromanaged level, the world appears to me to be governed by a higher spirit, one that influences your destiny before you are born. That's not to say you don't have any choice in the whole thing, but there seem to be powerful forces that shape who we become. It's not so much by roles or scripts that we assume, but paths that we follow that are carved by those before us. These paths are not necessarily clearly defined or well-marked, and they venture near treacherous chasms both psychic and corporeal. I've not led a reckless life, yet I've had five brushes with death, ones that yielded to me by a split-second change of course, or fraction of distance. Those fortuitous events tend to remain in your subconscious, as some hidden markers that remind you how tenuous and important the fragile adventure of life suspends in the balance. I've often wondered about the things I've had no control over and the what-ifs: had my mother made different decisions, had we not moved out of the city, had the neighbor kid's father not taken me up to their mountain camp where I caught the most gorgeous wild brookies. There's this gnawing notion in me that in the great scheme of things, there's more to it than how you play the hand you're dealt. It helps to appreciate that you may have wildcards scattered into the mix.

Not far from the home where I spent my boyhood, along the Neshaminy Creek, is a rock formation that juts out past the bank to offer an overlook affording a wider, more expansive view, both upstream and down. Local kids who first took me there unimaginatively dubbed it "Plymouth Rock," I suppose as a way of having it represent originality, the way the real one in Massachusetts is credited as the stepping-stone for Europeans who first arrived. Our Plymouth Rock, though, was a place of meditation, though we didn't call it that as kids. It was where you could get lost in thought, mesmerized by the sweeping flows parting around the only large boulders the stream offered in this section of water. I spent a lot of time alone there. For me it became a place of shelter, a harbor of safety from turbulent seas of the psyche thrashing the spirit of a young boy. Along the way, I've found similar rocks along other rivers, and have come to associate such places with healing forces if you just take the time to know them. In some ways, my path to fly-fishing has been an extension of my desire to wade among these rugged boulders to borrow some of their quiet strength.

*　　　*　　　*　　　*　　　*　　　*　　　*

The Neshaminy Creek is an unremarkable stream that flows from the lower Piedmont Plateau to the Coastal Plain in southeastern Pennsylvania before emptying into the Delaware River near Croydon. It is named for the indigenous tribe that inhabited the region before the arrival of European settlers. Eventually, the stream was dammed in many places as part of the Industrial Revolution to provide power for mills that sprung up along its course. Today it flows through suburban sprawl, receiving runoff from mall parking lots and shopping centers, rather than wetlands and bogs, to augment its volume. About two miles before it becomes tidal water, the Neshaminy is sizable at about 100 feet wide with a succession of large pools connected by gentle eddies and swift runs. I haven't fished it in more than twenty-five years even though it is my natal stream.

I vividly remember the first time I went down to that stream on my own. I was eight years old and had never fished before nor had ever known fishing. The calm, bright July afternoon was framed with a certain stillness usually observed later in the evening, as if an imperceptible curtain shielded the place from unwanted intrusion. I made my way down to "The Steps," a place where a local resident layered large, flat rocks descending to the water's edge as an easy entrance to a swimming hole. The last rock, perched on pilings of smaller boulders, was over four feet in length and nearly as wide. I dropped my towel on it next to the orange, plastic bucket I brought with me as I kicked off my faded sneakers. A feeling of pervasive emptiness enveloped the pool outstretched before me, as if my soul alone was to be present for some prearranged ritual. I slowly ventured into the alluring water, foam specks drifting lazily past me in the calm pool, carefully edging toward the bedrock that stretched to the center of the stream. The stream was unusually clear, perfect for a solitary baptism. In up to my knees, I stood very still and peered through the surface to search for signs of movement. Small minnows were tugging at the hairs on my legs. These annoying, brazen little creatures were daring me to scoop them up with my little plastic bucket. As I positioned myself carefully with the bucket tilted toward the water, ready for my first catch, I spied a much bigger fare that came into view from the corner of my eye. A striking, emerald sunfish with a bright orange underside, phosphorus glow, and a dark spot etched on his gently moving gill appeared before me. He inched closer to me while his fins undulated slowly forward to back, the way a fish might tread water. The pesky minnows kept after my leg hairs as I focused harder to block out their distracting nibbles and slowly turned toward my game. He was about an arm's length beyond my reach, and we stared at each other a very long time. I dared to inch closer. Fortunately, he didn't move. Very slowly, I raised the bucket to my side, pointing its mouth directly at the fish. He still didn't move. I was not conscious of anything around me. My total concentration dwelled on the capture of this gorgeous, foreign creature. With my little bucket readied by my side, I was poised over him. He was right under me, shifting closer to my knobby, submerged knees. Instinctively, I knew there was a right moment to strike. Timing was everything; I just needed to wait another second to keep him unsuspecting of my intentions until I was ready. A mental picture of the bucket plunging quickly into the water formed right before I did it. Swoosh! The impact destroyed the calm of the pool. The water in the bucket lapped the sides vigorously several times before it settled enough for me to see. I stared into the bucket, then into the ripples where I last saw the fish, finding him in neither. With lightning speed, he had escaped my best effort.

I was suddenly in awe of this wild creature who trusted me enough to share his presence for those precious moments. Instead of being satisfied with that, I tried to make him mine. But far from being disappointed, I was captured by the intrigue of this mysterious event. I found myself being trapped by an enduring magical web that enmeshes its victim the more it tries to escape. At this moment, I was blessed and cursed by the spell of the fishing passion.

3

Siren of Shangri-La

Love is a hard thing to master. It requires a great deal of self-reflection and awareness. The less emotional complexity you bring to a relationship, the better able you are to meld with the other person for a joyful shared ride through the universe. I am not one to give advice about love, however. By 1975, I had had a couple of live-in girlfriends, but the relationships fell apart after a year and a half. It seems for a lot of men, sex gets in the way of love sometimes, like having dessert before the main course. I should have paid more attention to the appetizers. Neither of those women shared interests that I had. I never bothered to really examine what I was looking for in a partner. And, of course, I brought my share of excess baggage. Woodstock Girl was different. We met at the Mummer's Parade in Philadelphia in 1976 and hit it off immediately. I call her Woodstock Girl because she had a cameo appearance in the film of the generation-defining concert of 1969. It was the scene where naked hippies are splashing each other playfully while rowing a surfboard across a large pond. She was tall, with long legs and wavy, auburn hair, breasts firm and ample. Being of Irish descent with lightly freckled apple cheeks and a pleasant smile, she would be described by most as pretty. I thought of her as lovely, if you can discern the difference. Everything we did together meshed well. I wasn't much in to fly-fishing at the time, but she was outdoorsy. We took many hikes where she would identify birds and wildflowers with great accuracy and passion. I bought binoculars and made a life list to keep up with her. We never argued about anything. But she shared a dark secret with me that unnerved my emotional compass. There were signs that intimacy might be hard for her, that her psychic wounds might hold her back. It gnawed at me. She tried counseling, but I thought she ended it too soon. Instead of supporting and comforting her, I tried to rip the bandages from the lesions in one rapid tear. Of course, I had my own issues. You do not get raised by a strict, demanding, seemingly uncaring father without it causing your own slips and falls. I called off the relationship.

After two years of occasionally dating other women, I reached out to her again in the spring of 1978. I resolved some of my own issues through therapy, and I was ready for a committed relationship. She reciprocated. Only I reached out at the wrong time. Work became dramatic, as state investigations were closing in where I was employed. I got so caught up in the turmoil that I neglected to call her for three weeks. She summoned me to her apartment, dressed me down, and then tossed me out of her life. At least that's how I remember it. I felt confused and numb, ashamed and paralyzed. Like I said, I'm not one to offer advice about love.

At the end of that summer, I was offered a job at a community college in a nearby city. A fresh start would be the best for my psyche at this point, so I decided to clear my head with a trip to Penns Creek. I knew nothing about the stream other than that it was famous, supposedly held lots of trout, and was 150 miles from the city. After throwing my camping gear in the trunk, I went up the steps of my Mt. Airy trinity rowhouse to lock the front door. In the car, I unfolded a tattered highway map and laid it on the passenger seat for one last look. Philadelphia basically has two seasons: hot concrete and cold concrete. August is, of course, the hot concrete season. It was 9am and I was already perspiring from the sweltering heat and felt relieved that I was finally heading off to the country. A gust of baking wind lifted scraps of street litter past the windshield as I started the engine of my 1967 Dodge Dart, one of the most reliable vehicles of its era. Steering opposite the morning rush-hour traffic, I passed familiar landmarks that gave me a sense of neighborhood: the Korean fish market, where I bought fresh, pan-ready sea bass; Hermann Brothers, a disheveled hardware store so chaotic only the two half-crazy brothers who operated it could find things, but stocked well enough that I could get just about anything I needed after listening to their inane diatribes; and the school for the deaf, a vast campus where silent recess was punctuated by the swiftly moving hands and fingers of exuberant cherubs under the watchful eye of solemn teachers who stood like mannequins at the edges of the playground. I welcomed the changes in scenery from the rowhouse neighborhoods of the city to tree-lined suburbs to the rolling hills of the South Mountain outside of Reading and finally to the Blue Ridge just north of Harrisburg. Once on the open highway, I embraced my journey, turning up the radio while the wind churned my long, wavy hair into unkempt tangles.

My artist, writer, and musician friends who fermented at the bottom fringes of urban culture knew little of my fishing exploits. Though having lived in the city proper for several years, I still held on to my fishing equipment—a spinning rod, some lures, and assorted tackle. It wasn't until I was twenty-five that I latched on to my first fly rod, a serviceable five-weight Browning fiberglass affair bought from a now-defunct sporting goods store located in Center City. My only lesson came from a self-described, downwardly mobile graduate of Goddard College in Vermont. Apparently, he spent most of his non-studious life fly-fishing the local streams and rivers of Plainfield. That one lesson involved using a nail knot to tie leader to the fly line and an improved clinch knot to secure the fly on to the tippet. We executed that lesson near Kitchens Lane on the Wissahickon Creek which bisects Fairmont Park in the northwest corner of Philadelphia. Though stocked with trout, we turned up none that day. Without waders though, I became adept at casting flies from the shrub-and tree-crowded banks as I often visited the Wissahickon after that. As you probably know, fly casting is front half skill of this craft. It took me nearly ten years of trial-and-error fumbling to accomplish the back half, knowing what to put on the end of the line to entice fish. I guess I was more invested in the art and grace of fly-fishing than preparing myself to be a competent fly angler.

After tooling on the road for about two hours, I followed the west rim of the Susquehanna north on Route 15, glancing every now and then at the river that the locals often describe as "a mile wide and a foot deep." It is a beautiful river and a renowned smallmouth bass destination— but not mine. Only a half-hour more of cruising would bring me to the edge of bliss. I did not consult my regulations booklet nor talked to anyone who had fished Penns Creek. It just seemed like a good idea to approach one of the state's best trout streams with an ample amount of obliviousness. Following the light-green route markings on my highway map, I made my way to the outskirts of Selinsgrove, the sleepy college town where the Susquehanna pinches Penns Creek. I figured that all I had to do was find that fabled stream and superb trout fishing would be mine to enjoy. Some back roads led me to what I expected were charmed waters. Steering with one eye on the stream and the other on the road, I pulled my fatigued Dodge over at the first pull-off I encountered, thinking that parking would be a premium on this well-regarded stream. My fingers fumbled with the keys as I hastily opened the trunk. Pausing for a moment, I decided to reach for the fly rod, freed it from the tube, and proudly inspected the best piece of fishing equipment I owned. The two sections fit together snugly, allowing me to quickly fasten the reel and string the leader through the guides. After all that time on the road, I could not contain the urge to fish any longer. I traced the clear path down to the grassy bank where I came to a sudden halt on the worn edges.

I should have suspected something after seeing the availability of parking. This place was mine alone. My first time on that stream was ignorance multiplied by stupidity. I had ample places to fish since the majority of that portion of the stream bottom revealed a mix of sand and pebbles with clumps of elodea swaying in the current. That day in late August, when the leaves were hinting at fall despite the warm, bright sun glaring on the lazy currents, I was twenty miles below the venerable trout infested water that makes Penns Creek a premier destination for many eastern anglers. There were only about eight weeks between this day and the end of the notorious Green Drake hatch. At the time, I wouldn't have recognized a Green Drake from a Black Gnat, of course, since I knew nothing of aquatic insects or trout flies. My fly box consisted of "fabulous trout fly selections" hustled to all unsuspecting beginners by mail-order fly shops. Little did I know that a #14 Light Hendrickson wasn't going to attract a mutant mosquito, let alone a suspicious fish. So I tied one on. I cast it out to the middle of the stream and watched as small shiners suddenly appeared as tiny, fitful forms nervously establishing a pecking order behind that silly fly. Several bumped it with their noses, but it was too big to be taken into their pouting mouths. I cast again farther upstream and then down. After a few attempts to lure larger fare in some faster runs, I packed up and moved farther downstream in hopes of finding deeper water.

The lower proved to be only a bit more productive. I spied a few splashy rises which I thought were trout. There was some scant success with the fly rod, but it wasn't how Ted Trueblood described it in *Outdoor Life*. Five-inch sunfish assaulted the fly ferociously, but trout were not to be my destiny, not this day anyway. Feeling somewhat defeated after an hour of fishing, I decided to find a campground for the evening. The map denoted a red teepee aside the torn crease, the symbol for camping. I could not tell if it was public or private, but it appeared close enough to give a try. Buzzing along the back-country roads, I motored around a sharp bend before encountering an entrance with the enchanting "Shangri-La Camping Resort" carved on the hand-hewn log gate. It hardly looked like or had the feel of the mythical utopia of Hilton's *Lost Horizon*. The place was nearly deserted, which seemed a little unusual for the week before Labor Day. The old gent at the check-in put me on the edge of a large, wooded expanse next to an open field of sunbaked ground where an odd assortment of weeds and grasses did battle for control of what was once a dusty cornfield. Driving over to my assigned space, I parked and got out to look around. The fire ring was tucked in a tree-shaded area not far from shower facilities and restrooms. A rustic picnic table straddled a low hump of naked ground. Feeling a bit tired, I took a moment to sit and cupped my hands to my face. Fly-fishing, like love, was a bit more complicated than I had expected.

As I unpacked, I glanced around at the other sites, searching for any signs of activity. About thirty yards from me an old, gray, two-person tent stood pitched on a dry, level berm at the edge of a slow-moving stream. Next to it, a well-worn but proud-looking VW Bug with faded bumper stickers sat idly near their fire ring, as if a loyal pet waiting for its master. There were no other indications of who might be there, and after surveying the rest of the wooded expanse and seeing no other campers, I returned to the trunk of my car. I continued to unpack my meager belongings and searched for the reliable brown canvas pup tent I always brought on these kinds of trips. When I located it, I took it to level ground underneath the tree canopy and rolled it on to the firm, dry landing. I then searched for the stakes and twine that would help the tent take its humble form.

The stakes resisted the parched, solid ground, taking their hold feebly as I struggled to pound them in. Eventually the tent took shape, sagging helplessly over the center twine as I arranged the other equipment around the campsite. Washing up at the bath house seemed like a logical next step before starting dinner. While there, I heard the shower running on the other side, the women's side. It was the only other hint that someone else was at the campground. Back at the campsite, I set up a portable Hibachi on the picnic table and started to grill a chicken breast with sliced vegetables dressed in herbs, wrapped in foil. As the smoke was lifting off the grill, I turned and looked across the opening by the parked VW. Walking toward the other tent was a young woman with a shapely figure wearing an ankle-length, tight-fighting red robe with the hood drawn over her head. Caught a little off-guard, I felt I had to move around, mimicking that I was doing something so that it didn't appear that I was staring. Not wanting to appear rude, I was intrigued to know that an attractive woman was camped next door to a single and eligible fly-fishing dude. She disappeared into the tent. I speculated on whether she was alone or with someone. Some tangling nights would sure make up for fishless days, I fancied. Being single and free, I considered, has its upside at times like this.

Lost for the moment in lust-driven thought, I resumed my dinner preparations. With the charcoal fire humming, I opened the foil that contained the meal and pierced the chicken breast with a knife to see if it was done. It slid through easily and appeared on the underside of the slightly crisp, white meat. Juices trickled into the coals of the fire, splattering ashes askew. Carefully hoisting it off the grill on to a paper plate, I deftly unwrapped the foil from the vegetables and poured them next to the chicken. The juices from the vegetables and the meat mingled in the center of the plate, the herbal steam entering my nostrils, and I reminded myself that I had not eaten since I left the city early that morning. I took the knife and cut a piece off the chicken, chewing it slowly and savoring the taste for a long while. A carrot rolled to the side of the plate. I picked it up and licked its juices before chewing it to a pulp.

The sun slid behind the trees that bordered the campground. A gentle breeze started to stir as I rested my back against the edge of my picnic table to reflect. Having spent a great deal of time in the city exposed me to the gritty textures of big-city life. I often hung out in noisy dart bars where the juke box played blues house rockers like Muddy Waters, Sonny Boy Williamson, and Willie Dixon. This campground was lightyears from my urban existence. City life would seem foreign to folks living here. I doubted that most people in these parts visit art museums, go to symphonies, or ever ride subways. The countryside offered a respite from the shake and grind of urban rhythms, though I couldn't imagine the appeal of living here all the time.

An unexpected spate of activity churned in the stubble field next to the trees. I reached for my binoculars and the bird guidebook I had begun carrying on my fishing trips. Small ground birds flitted about in the dusk—chipping sparrows! A new bird for my list. I jotted it down in the field notes section. No fish today but a new bird. And just like that, my thoughts briefly drifted to Woodstock Girl. She would have been pleased by a new bird on the list, a personal, natural discovery that delights the mind and maybe eases the emotional scarring hidden in the depths of a fragile psyche. Our awkward separation a few months earlier kept haunting me, leaving me wondering what subconscious motive caused me to fail. I was unable to sort out my inability to explain to her my unintended absence that she so angrily and rightly demanded

I account for. Replaying my feeble replies to her left me feeling disordered. At that point, I felt I had to just let it go and hope that I learned something, but I am not sure I did. The chipping sparrows seemed not to care.

I reached for the bottle of wine that I was saving for dinner and clunked the fruity California chenin blanc on the picnic table. Feeling a sense of detachment, I poured the golden liquid into a glass. After a minute, the glass perspired from the chill cast by the wine. I looked through it and felt some quiet satisfaction at getting away for a fishing adventure in a remote, featureless campground miles upon miles away from the steamy city. This accidental destination was itself ample reward, I thought. It seemed befitting to be here in Shangri-La. I slowly finished the rest of the dinner and poured another glass of wine. Twilight ushered dusk on to the meadow, the last ambient light of this warm August day dimming slowly, casting an amber hue over the field. The stillness and vastness of the place gave me the feeling of an odd sense of timelessness, as if somehow, I had known I would have to come here.

My peace was suddenly interrupted by a rustling sound that was behind me. It was her, the woman from the tent. She was approaching me in an alluring fashion, still wearing the red robe. It was a one-piece pullover affair that clung tightly to her body, outlining the smooth curves of her wide, inviting hips as she moved toward me. Her breasts, large and firm, thrust themselves tautly, as if leading the rest of her body in a proud saunter. Her nipples jutted out, causing the material to misbehave seductively. I was taken back by her hair. At a time when most women were wearing long hair down to the middle of the back, she had shorn her blonde hair very short. It reminded me of the crew cuts I used to get as a kid. She was close now, so I made eye contact to get a sense of her being. High cheekbones accentuated her face. Well-formed pink lips underscored a sexy smile. My gaze tracked to her light-blue eyes. I found her attractive, and that made me nervous.

"Hi," I mustered. "I take it we're neighbors."

"Yeah. Nice night isn't it?" she replied.

"I was just admiring the colors across the field. The breeze feels good too."

"Mind if I sit down?" she asked.

"No, g-go right ahead," I blurted, unintentionally revealing my anxious tone. I offered her a glass of wine, hoping that she would accept.

"Sure, just one though."

She poured a glass of wine and smiled slightly as she looked up at me. Things were off to a good start, I thought. I introduced myself. She revealed only one name. There was something about her name, Blossom, that suggested an essence of herbs or fresh fruit—pure, creamy, even organic. She had a presence about her that seemed wholesome and open, quite unlike the women I encountered in the city who averted their glances or stared coldly forward whenever a man approached. It seems she went by only one name as part of some kind of personal transformation.

"I gave up my other name when I joined my spiritual community."

I hesitated before responding, trying to appear nonchalant, but her reply put me off-guard.

"Oh, really. What was it before?"

"I don't want to discuss it."

"I'm sorry."

"Our leader thinks we need to shed all identity from the past in order to become more in balance with the cosmic forces."

"Your leader?"

"Yes, Alexander. He's very wise."

"So, you follow his teachings or something?

"Yes. I took a vow of obedience to the teachings of a Higher Law."

I was getting an uneasy feeling from the mix of messages I was getting from her. I plodded on though.

"Where are you from?"

"Virginia. I came up here for the Vegetarian Conference at Susquehanna University."

Oh God, I thought, *a radical vegetarian cultist*. I had heard of these types before but had never come face-to-face with somebody whose being was given over to another person. It was hard for me to imagine letting someone else lay out your life's choices for you based on some philosophy that required conformity. I liked to learn about life first-hand, even if it meant making some mistakes along the way. She presented more complexity though. She was definitely sexy and seemed to want to reveal this part of herself. My thoughts returned to seduction. This was not going to be easy, I reckoned.

"Are you here for the conference?" she quizzed.

"No, I just came up from Philly to get away for a few days, do a little fishing maybe."

"Why would you want to do something like that?"

"Well, it's kind of hot in the city this time of year and--"

"No, I mean fishing," she interrupted, looking intensely disapproving. "It's awfully cruel."

"Oh, I don't keep them," I lied.

"That's even worse. You're tormenting those little creatures."

At this point I became very self-conscious. I needed a shower. Should I try to respond to her in some intelligent way? The whole opportunity was beginning to slip away. I wasn't connecting with her at all. I wondered if she slept with Alexander. Did she sleep with other men in the commune? Would she sleep with a smelly, meat-eating fisherman? *Oh, good God*, my inner voice proclaimed, *come to your senses, boy*.

"Well, they don't seem to mind, and anyway, I enjoy it."

"Enjoy it?" she responded, appearing incredulous. "I think you need to look at what you're doing. We weren't put here on this Earth to abuse animals."

"It's not abuse. Besides, neither of us would be here now if our ancestors didn't fish."

"It's not needed now. That's what answering to a Higher Law is all about."

I felt rankled by her strident tone. This was not going where I had hoped. I knew that vegetarians didn't relish eating meat and all that, but what was this attack on fishing? It was part of the core of my being, like breathing, laughing, and sweating. Why didn't she just ask me to tear out my soul? I wasn't sure how to respond to her.

"What about plants? You eat carrots, lettuce, and such, right?" I quizzed, deciding to go on the offensive.

"That's not the same thing."

"Why is that?"

"They don't have feelings."

"So that's how you determine your stance with animals? Whether or not they get hurt?"

"Of course. I don't want to be responsible for their suffering."

I picked up a small dead branch and began scratching aimlessly in the bare patch of dirt between us, calculating my next move.

"What if I told you that the Russians have been doing some experiments with photographing auras of plants? They've done research in this, you know. Seems that if you talk to the plants harshly or threaten them with scissors, they cringe. At least, their auras shrivel."

"Well, I don't know about that."

"Well, I saw it recently in a science journal."

"So, what are you trying to say?" she queried.

"What I'm suggesting is that plants and all life have a perceptible 'life force' or aura that we can detect with instruments that are sensitive enough. And anything that is done to harm them is felt by them in some way, maybe not through nerve endings, but their own biological framework for detecting threats, pain, and even death."

Blossom sensed where I was going with this, and it looked as if she was beginning to feel uneasy. She folded her arms in front of her chest. I got up to close the flap to my tent. She crossed her legs, revealing her right thigh through the slit in her robe. As I returned to the bench, I feigned looking past her as I focused in on her legs. I could see the light-blonde, wispy hairs leaning across her smooth, peachy skin. She didn't shave her legs—that was obvious—and in a strange way it added to her allure. I gave serious thought to a chance encounter that might lead to something more intimate, but I was focused on this unexpected challenge to my beliefs and didn't care how I came across. This was no longer about a sexual liaison, but about who I was and my interpretation of the world. My senses were heightened by her provocations. I could see Blossom reacting to my emerging passion. She watched me carefully as I leaned across the table. My chest muscles tightened under my snug t-shirt. My back straightened, adding intensity to my demeanor, like an athlete ready to go into a game. I lit a candle that was in the middle of the table. Surely, she had other handsome lovers before she became affiliated with the commune. I guessed Blossom could never connect with them on the spiritual level that she determined to be an important part of her essence. I think she could see that I did not believe as she did, but I was perhaps an astute opponent, maybe different than the others. Using this pause, she tried to deflect me.

"Why can't you just enjoy nature by watching it?"

My eyes widened. I measured my thoughts carefully before responding to her. The candle on the table started to flicker as a cool breeze swept across the meadow.

"Well, let me put it this way. You recognize that many people worship their deity in a distinct and personal way, much like yourself, right?"

"Yes, I suppose, but what's that got to do with it?"

"Well, I respect that, and I even respect that your Higher Spirit, who maybe speaks to you through Alexander, is sending a message to you about your relationship with the other beings on this mysterious planet of ours. But it sounds like your supreme being is not so proud of the lesser creatures that have been created. It seems it allows you to draw lines to define your place with those beings so that you can exploit some, but animals have a higher standing and can't be viewed in the same way. My God makes no such distinctions. He...or maybe She...or It, is a God that blesses all creations with equal warmth and passion and gives them an unwavering sense of survival. We happen to be fortunate enough to be able to exercise our will with the other creatures most of the time. For me, that means I don't draw lines, and I don't view my connection with them as strictly exploitive or in some hierarchy, but rather a respectful appreciation of the interdependence that we share. It's like when our native people hunted game; they always made a brief offering of gratitude to the Great Spirit before the animal was slain. In that same vein, when I put a sunfish back in the stream, I revere his meager existence enough to make me want to let him live out his destiny without my further interference. And when I eat a handsome trout, I make a sacred choice about my survival and my being that overrides his in the same way that you and I make similar kinds of unconscious choices every time we park a car in a field, pluck a ripened berry from a vine, or even say something to another. If we were to extend your beliefs about animals to all living creatures, we would just shrivel up and die. I don't think the Creative Spirit intends for either of us to do that. What we have to do is weigh the outcome of our actions against the possible detriment to all creatures and live within ourselves the best we can and be judged later. To my way of thinking, we need to influence people more in their relationships with others, since it's there that we have so many more choices yet cause so much more pain."

Blossom stared intently at me. I guessed my demeanor reminded her of Alexander, my passion as compelling. I got the feeling that my thoughtful, deliberate responses to her strongly held beliefs made me an adversary. Not a good way to form a relationship. She wasn't going to get a sympathetic convert and I was losing the mood for carnal intimacy. I'm sure she knew that she started out enticing me with her sensuous movements and graceful demeanor. Certainly she had that power over men her whole adult life. Perhaps she had misjudged me. I wasn't sure of her intentions when she wandered over to my campsite. Was she looking for a lover? A convert? Forming a relationship? I think our encounter set her back. She was probably used to getting what she wanted. The lustful side of me wanted to go along with her persuasions. She finished her wine and set the glass down.

"Well Lou, I don't know where to begin. I need more time to think about what you said. You made some very good points. My teachings with Alexander have led me to a different understanding of nature, but I'd like to explore this with you further. Perhaps we can pick this up again tomorrow night?"

"Maybe, if I decide to stay around here another day," I replied. "I was thinking of heading down river tomorrow, over to Sherman's Creek." My mind quickly shifted from lust, to love, to committed relationship. It was the latter that I was interested in. I was hoping to find it with Woodstock Girl. We had so much more in common. It was obvious that anything with Blossom was going to be contentious around food and fishing. You know, the basics. Meanwhile she unfolded her arms, straightened her back, and shifted her hips at the same time, focusing her gaze directly into my eyes.

"Well, I'll be here if you care to get together. You may even want to go over to the conference with me. Maybe then we'll have more time to talk, and I can give you a better understanding of why I feel the way I do. So listen, I won't bother you any more tonight. Goodnight."

"And to you too," I replied.

With that, Blossom got up from the table and went back toward her tent. The light from the candle splashed on her rear. The tight-fitting robe revealed the contours of her nice, firm ass. She swayed gracefully as each cheek took prominence when she took a new step. I smiled faintly to myself as she disappeared into the blanket of darkness, then got up and walked over to my car. Leaning against it, I gazed into the night sky. This time I did not let lust fuzz up whatever might lead to finding a soul mate. But life and love are both about learning the hard way sometimes. Sherman's Creek called to me to come see her next. Who knew what lessons might await there?

4

Tulpehocken Dreams

The mid-July morning had a slight chill to it as I made my way down to the Refrigerator Pool from the Rebers Bridge parking lot. Surprisingly, there were few anglers on the water that morning for the thick trico hatch that was just starting to come off. Within a half-hour a dense cloud of the dainty, black mayflies with translucent wings softly vibrated about thirty feet above the stream. Within another half-hour, the spent duns started tumbling on the water in dense mats. The trout were waiting for them, and the first dimples signaled the beginning of the feast, tiny hors d'oeurves coursing down the foam line of the Tulpehocken Creek as I positioned myself at the tail of the pool. A waterlogged branch about five inches in diameter wedged itself between a pair of boulders, its tail-end wobbling methodically in the eddy below, causing the current to curl and eventually disperse the tiny flies behind the branch in such a way that four or five large brown trout set up behind each other, intercepting several flies at a time. After watching for a few minutes, I tied a size #24 imitation to my 7X tippet and began working the seam, focusing on the last trout in the line. By now the blue sky turned to a filmy, gray mist dripping with slick, tiny, black bodies. Being present for this phenomenon felt like a gift, a blessing.

There were so many insects on the water that it was hard to determine my fly among the drift. Each dimple looked like a sure take, so I often pulled back to what amounted to a plethora of false hits. Eventually I tagged the trailing trout—about fifteen inches—that I was able to lead away from the pack without disturbing the other feeders. Within five minutes I took another healthy fourteen-inch brown. After the water settled, the others moved up in position like skiers in line waiting for the next lift. Two more browns appeared at the end of that same seam. As I looked farther downstream, the next pool was also bustling with feeding trout as was the head of the Refrigerator Pool. Spent spinners and fish were everywhere. It looked and felt like the Nirvana of fly-fishing. As I was about to make my next cast, voices from upstream penetrated the quiet of the morning; a group of four anglers headed toward me. One by one, they emerged from around a bend, approaching the gravel bar ahead of the pool. By their conversations I could tell they had just arrived and had not wet their lines yet. When they were about thirty yards from me they stopped and spaced themselves out evenly. Seeing all the fish rising whetted their desire to get started, but I could see immediately that they would not be successful. All four were carrying spinning rods. That section of the Tulpehocken permits artificial lures as well as flies with a delayed harvest. They were within their rights to try for these trout, but it was pretty obvious from their conversations and gear that it was their first time on the Tulpehocken Creek.

It went something like this:

"Look at all those trout."

"Yeah, just pick one out and sling your lure past him."

Then to this:

"They're not even looking at it."

"Right. Just gorging on those tiny little flies on the water."

To:

"I think that guy down there has the answer."

"That's the third nice fish he's caught since we've been here. Gotta bring a fly rod here."

They left after about 20 minutes with nary a hit or follow. I, of course, was the "guy down there" and would have gladly shared all the technical details necessary to catch trout on July mornings on the Tulpehocken. I do think a couple of fly-curious fishermen were among that bunch. I was one of them a dozen years earlier.

*   *   *   *   *   *   *

The Tulpehocken Creek rises at the eastern edge of Lebanon County in southeastern Pennsylvania as a spring creek, just east of the city of Lebanon. The stream is one of the larger tributaries of the Schuylkill River. In colonial times, the Union Canal paralleled its length to bridge the Delaware and Susquehanna watersheds for the movement of goods in the early days of commerce. It flows through a wide swath of agriculture lands where it is quickly degraded by poor farming practices producing silt, higher temperatures, and minimal riparian vegetation that quickly compromise its trout-carrying capacity. In recent years the Tulpehocken Chapter of Trout Unlimited, along with other local partners, has initiated an aggressive campaign to convince farmers to fence off cattle and provide riparian space between pastured or cultivated fields to recover the stream. In a place where pinching pennies is an expectation and even considered a genetic disposition, it can be a hard sell to ask farmers to give up even eight feet of buffer for conservation efforts. But as I found later in my own conservation efforts, any healthy riparian buffer is better than none, so protection efforts persist in that watershed because it is so necessary to a vibrant fishery.

But I am getting ahead of myself, so let me drift further back in time. In June of 1972, the remnants of Hurricane Agnes unleashed horrific flooding on eastern and central Pennsylvania. The city of Reading, along with other downstream municipalities, was inundated by the Schuylkill River, causing millions of dollars in damage and large-scale evacuations. Like many other places at the time, politicians in Pennsylvania sought to restrain rivers to manage flooding so the Army Corps of Engineers was commissioned to construct a dam for a flood control reservoir on the Tulpehocken Creek a few miles above Reading. In 1979, the Blue Marsh Dam was completed with a bottom release feature. In short time it became obvious that a high-quality tailwater trout fishery was possible. The flows and hatches were mostly predictable, depending upon the month, making the stream equivalent to a large spring creek in many respects. Parallel to the construction of the dam, the Tulpehocken Chapter of Trout Unlimited was formed in 1976, and the chapter has been the primary fisheries advocate for the stream ever since. Partnering with the Pennsylvania Fish and Boat Commission, the TU chapter advanced the planting of fingerling trout as opposed to adult "catchable" trout (i.e. 8-12-inch fish) to spur a fishery more akin to wild fish than typical stocked streams. It was the development of this fishery that put the Tulpehocken on the map and made it a destination, not only for local anglers, but for many within a fifty-mile radius. Having lived some thirty-five miles away in Schwenksville at the time, I was one of the invaders. I fished it so often that it became my adopted "home waters" even though the Perkiomen Creek was literally steps from my front door. The Tully, as it is affectionately referred to by locals, gave me my fly-fishing education, but my journey to that stream started much earlier.

The first trout I ever caught was a wild brook trout, about seven or eight inches of the most beautiful fish in the state. In fact, I caught a half-dozen of them in an unnamed tributary to Cedar Run in Tioga County Pennsylvania when I was nine years old. I was lucky enough to have a neighbor whose family shared a hunting camp in a remote location near the unincorporated village of Leetonia. I had never before been to a mountainous area (though Pennsylvania "mountains" would be called foothills anywhere else). The father of this family both fished and hunted and had many stories about experiences at the camp. We took a day from the camp and went to Big Pine Creek where he plied a bamboo fly rod. I had never seen a rod like that, but I must admit to being mildly intrigued. Meanwhile his son, my friend and baseball teammate, and I tossed C.P. Swings. None of us caught trout, but very tiny smallmouth bass thought the flies and the lures were tasty morsels and we caught many of them. The brookies were caught on the tributary across from the camp. They were just as eager as the bass, with small earthworms the bait of choice. Dapping into plunge pools entailed the angling technique. Between the both of us we caught eight small brookies that were carted on ice back home for a fish-fry the next day. I remember the fish having delectable, tender, pink flesh.

Most of my early fishing was done on the Neshaminy Creek near the village of Hulmeville. The Neshaminy may have been a trout stream 400 years ago, but logging, agriculture, and dams ruined everything by the beginning of the nineteenth century. By the middle of the twentieth century suburban sprawl, with its attendant runoff, converted it to a warm-water fishery where small and large mouth bass became the game fish of choice, though bluegills, crappies, fallfish, and catfish made for good sport for novice fishermen. The PA Fish and Boat Commission did stock trout in the Neshaminy well above the borough of Langhorne, but most of those fish disappeared within a few weeks of opening day, taken by eager anglers in search of fresh-caught dinner. I even got my share in one or two trips there as a teen. By the first of June, the water was lethal to any that escaped the onslaught of lures and baited hooks.

If there is one person to blame for instigating my fly-fishing passion, I'll have to point to Ted Trueblood. I recall stealthily reading articles from popular sporting magazines as a twelve-year-old while he described trekking through the Rockies plying a fly rod. A Colorado Spinner, a cross between a lure and a fly, was often at the business end of the tippet. Today that fly is considered a vintage collectible, but Ted swore by its effectiveness, and it probably was in lightly fished rivers of Idaho and Montana. On the Tulpehocken today, the trout would laugh at it.

*   *   *   *   *   *   *

"They're taking caddis, about a size 16."

One of the many kind anglers I encountered on the Tulpehocken pitched that advice after he saw me putting away my rod with that exasperated look that fishermen take on when they are bewildered. It qualified as my first lesson on the Tully and maybe my first lesson in entomology as well. It told me that buying a box of a dozen "starter flies" from a well-known mail-order retailer was not the way to solve the trout-catching problem. I certainly tried all twelve of them. I think I could almost hear the smirking of the trout as they ignored all the offerings I made in my first couple of visits to that stream. Even though I had owned a fly rod for a dozen years, visiting the Tulpehocken made me realize I was a fly-fishing novitiate. I looked up caddis and bought a half-dozen in the size the guy mentioned; lo and behold, on that next visit I had action: many "refusals" and a couple of brown trout. Made my day, and like winning at the racetrack the first time you go, it ignited what might be loosely described as an addiction, though in polite company we'd call it a passion. The size-16 caddis dry fly worked well in May, but as the season progressed, the size of the caddis became more diminutive, #18 by the beginning of June and #22 by the end. Then the tricos, a hatch of tiny mayflies that swarmed in thick clouds till about the beginning of August when things tapered off till about the middle of September when tricos resumed. Size #24 and #26 solved most hatch conditions and 7X and 8X tippets were the necessary norm. This was, as they say, technical fishing, exacting in fly choice and size, tippet diameter, and casting acumen. Midges round out the most prominent hatches, those occurring between the beginning of December through the beginning of April. There are other minor hatches that can turn up fish—Sulphurs in late May and flying ants and Yellow Drakes in September are among the other hatches that I encountered. No wild trout were reproducing but planted fall fingerling trout were growing quickly and taking on many of the traits of wild fish. They could be secretive at times and the carryover from year to year was consistently good. A third-year fish could measure 14-17-inches. The rainbows performed aerial displays when hooked, and the browns fought like, well, hefty browns. As they aged, the fish became smarter from all the previous hook-ups, so larger fish were also educated fish. By my third year on the Tully, I was experienced enough to be in the game on every visit.

One of my most memorable trips to the Tully occurred around the Mother's Day caddis hatch in the spring of 1987. This is the middle of what I call the Golden Age of the tailwater. As one visitor from upstate commented, these fish liked to "look up." Dry fly-fishing could attract a fair number of fish if the fly were exacting in size and color. It did not necessarily mean you were going to catch a lot of fish, as the Tully became an extremely popular place for fly anglers in eastern Pennsylvania. The fish had been pinched enough times that they became sophisticated, particularly if you fished exclusively dries as I did at that time. The pressure was becoming heavy as the word spread, so solitude was not one of the primary experiences, but there was enough room that anglers could spread out for a quality occasion most days. That caddis hatch not only brought up slashing trout but more determined anglers like myself. It was and still is the feature hatch of the stream.

That particular morning in May greeted me with a soft day, high wispy clouds marring a faded, blue sky with hardly any breeze. I parked by the Paper Mill Pool, surprised that I was the only one in that spot. The Paper Mill Pool is a mostly placid flat with a supple run at the head. Trout always park at the head of the pool to intercept caddis when they are coming off. From the bank I could see determined rises, not splashy but noticeably direct intercepts of emerging bugs. Several fish in the 12-14-inch range were working steadily, undisturbed by my gentle wading to reach them. I took three almost immediately before the rest moved on, obviously a bit ticked-off by all the commotion. I waded above the run, about 100 yards, where a nice seam holds fish below a stove-size boulder. Three more came to hand. The hatch was steady, not strong, but not dissipating either. I went after a few more fish farther upstream before deciding to head down to the Road to Nowhere bridge. About 150 yards below the bridge, a deep run meets a large pool. More fish were rising in the run. I'd taken another half dozen there, the largest was maybe 15 inches, a muscular rainbow with a solid, crimson, lateral stripe. All fish so far caught on the same fly, surprisingly not a single break-off. After forty-five minutes or so, the hatch started to dissipate. I saw maybe a half-dozen anglers total in the two-plus hours that I fished, which seemed low considering the popularity of the hatch and the pleasantness of the day. At that time I did not wear a vest but instead shouldered an orange knapsack containing my fly boxes, tippet, assorted supplies, and of course, my lunch. While standing knee-deep in the water, I would spin the knapsack around to fetch a peanut butter and jelly sandwich, eating as I cast with one hand. No more fish were willing, but since it was such a successful day, I decided to try one more spot, a place where I had never gone before but heard about from other anglers.

The Waterworks parking location is accessed by a dirt and gravel drive just north of the Western Berks Water Authority, a treatment facility that syphons water below the Blue Marsh Dam and distributes treated water to several municipalities in the region. I found out on this magical caddis day that it is likely the most popular location on the creek. There were at least a dozen cars squeezed in every available spot when I arrived at the bottom of the drive. That alone almost made me want to turn around. At the same time, a truck was leaving one of the coveted spaces, so I jumped into the space if for no other reason than to get a look at the water. A rugged path led down a gulley to a short stretch of bank. Lugging my rod, I looked to my right and could see the intake of the Water Authority about 100 yards downstream. Two low, long pools spaced apart by a short glide revealed no fish working. And no anglers present. To my left, six or seven anglers were working the 150-yard stretch of glides and riffles of more promising water. On the bank high above the stream were a gaggle of on-lookers, likely fishers who had ended their session but were acting as a kind of cheering section for those still flogging water. There wasn't much left to cheer, it seemed. In the last glide, occasional fish were taking emergers, as the hatch by now had died down considerably. The last submerged boulder in that glide divided the current, making a dry fly hard to present. Since they were the only fish not being cast to, I decided to cross the stream and circle around the boulder for a better casting position. I kept looking upstream as I progressed across the stream to check on the other anglers, but no one was hooking fish. I'll say this now because it applies almost every time I fish. I prefer solitude and when I have to fish among others, I never do well. Perhaps it is some form of performance anxiety that is unconsciously transmitted down the line, but fish seem to read my vibes and let my flies alone. So my expectations were low. It was a new section on the Tully for me and I had already had a fabulous day. My adopted home waters turned out to be the dream stream of my fly-fishing existence. Being present was good enough. I was sure that the horde of anglers who fished earlier in the day pummeled the fish by that last boulder, and they were cautious about what was floating above them. The same fly that worked downstream earlier in the day stayed on my tippet. Three trout were still working sporadically when I prepared my first cast. A too-short presentation slid harmlessly away from the closest fish, the one positioned above the other two. Pulling out another foot of line from my reel, I cast above the boulder again. The extra bit of slack allowed the fly to drift closer to the boulder. In an instant, a solid take straightened my tippet. Fish on, and a sizeable one at that. I played him for a few minutes before securing the fish in my left hand. A fat 14-inch brown gave me that look that seemed as if he was more surprised than I was. I could hear a few murmurs from the high bank as I release the fish. After a morning tearing into fish, my fly was a bit beat-up and now water-logged. The last two fish started working again behind the boulder after the catch disturbance. My futile efforts to air dry the fly by false casting suggested I might be done for the day. I had more of these flies in my box but did not feel it was necessary to break it open for the last hurrah, so I flipped the soaked fly practically on top of the submerged boulder and watched it sink almost immediately. In an instant, my line tightened. Another hefty trout started tugging and splashing. The cheering section stared, seemingly astounded, as I played this fish. I could barely make out the words, but it sounded like, "I've seen that guy with the knapsack before, usually down below." It was more attention than I usually garner while fishing, but my facade of nonchalance covered an internal buoyance. I was killing it in pretty tough circumstances. As I was finally unhooking the thick-shouldered brown, I could hear the audible whisper of one of the upstream anglers to his close partner, "Why don't you ask him what he is using?" Of course, he didn't, but both continued to look on. At that point it seemed like I was the only one fishing. I paid no attention to what else was happening on the water. Basketball players refer to this as being "in the zone," those moments on the court where you play on an unconscious level, making every shot close in or out on the perimeter. Not sure if fishing calls up a similar analogy, but I was without a doubt "in the zone." By now, my success appeared almost absurd. I was having my best day ever on the Tully, or anywhere. The stream seemed magical. Casts were falling into place, fly selection was perfect, and conditions were ripe. It could not be a better place to fish, and I could do no wrong. I stood still for several minutes until the water settled. I knew there was one more working fish, and I almost felt embarrassed trying for him, but I flipped the soaked fly one last time and sure enough, the last working fish in that section took. After I released that fish, I kept my head down, circled back to the bank. and marched directly to the truck feeling partly ashamed for my gluttony, partly ecstatic for my great success, and wholly detached from everything and everybody.

Epilogue: The fly was a Kings River Caddis. It imitates a spotted sedge found locally in the Kings River, a California stream originating in the Sierra Mountains and flowing west toward Fresno. The fly was developed by Wayne "Buz" Buszek of Visalia, California. I don't remember where I bought the flies (I was not tying at the time), but after that wondrous day on the Tully I went back the next weekend thinking I had discovered the Holy Grail of caddis flies. I fished for five hours, tossed the fly over many rising fish and caught only one gullible 8-inch brown. The fly never performed again like that one day, and I hardly ever went to it after that.

*   *   *   *   *   *   *

I rarely make travel plans for Labor Day weekend and this particular holiday was no different. After some time spent gardening, the cool morning gave way to a pleasant afternoon in the low 80s, blue sky guaranteed. It was not the best time to fish, but you know the adage. The place I chose on the Tully that day was one that I first visited when I discovered the stream, but one I had not selected in quite some time, a year or two perhaps. Downstream of the stilling basin of the Blue Marsh Dam starts the special regulation waters. There are several nice pools and glides before the deflectors installed by the Tulpehocken Chapter of Trout Unlimited appear on the north bank of the stream. If there was ever an apt synonym for TU members of that chapter, "rock throwers" quickly comes to mind, especially back then. As their home stream, the chapter went to great pains to improve flow below the dam, and the deflectors became the signature project of the early work of the chapter. I decided to set up at the pool before the first deflector. On the north side, the bank meets a level floodplain with a mix of sycamores, oaks, and maples on the flat terrain. On the south bank (the one I would be casting toward), a steep embankment of 100 feet or more met the water's edge, causing the trees on that side to lean over the water, offering a slice of shade on the water that would otherwise reflect the strong, warm sun. My expectations were low. No fish were rising, and this was one of the few times I spurned a dry fly in favor of a nymph, an all-purpose, brown-bodied variety with that "buggy" look that seems to interest fish when nothing else will. I waded out about one-third of the way across the stream. The shade reached out about four feet from the bank. The current was slow along the edge, disturbed by a small boulder almost touching the bank. If there was ever a trout hiding place, that would be it. A few false casts allowed me to place the fly the right distance, but the subtle current swirls would not allow the fly to sweep past the boulder close enough. I shifted my position little more upstream and closer to the south bank. When I settled my feet, I heard a series of deep chirps, then a short silence followed by a few more chirps. It was distinctive and I had heard it before. I looked downstream and to my left. On that north bank, about 75 yards below, stood a dead sycamore. Perched atop was a handsome osprey, obviously in migration but close to a reliable food source. Nice addition to the moment, the kind of natural experience that makes fishing enjoyable even when the fish aren't biting. Looking to my right, I spied a canoe with two occupants about 100 yards upstream, heading my way. They must have just launched by the stilling basin. I figured I had maybe two or three more casts before they would be close enough to disturb the action. Another cast produced no take, but the fly was closer to my intended target. I looked over my shoulder again. The canoe was closer but there was still time for another cast or two if there was a trout behind that boulder. With just one false cast, I dropped the fly about a foot above that boulder, so close to the bank I thought I might be in water too shallow to allow a drift without being snagged. After a second or two, the drift stopped, and a sharp tug caused me to pull back. In an instant, the water exploded. A sizable fish, maybe fifteen inches, broke the water. Clearly this rainbow was startled. He immediate swung away from the bank and headed downstream, ripping off line fast enough to cause a rumble in the reel seat. As this fish coursed to the middle of the stream, I glanced over my shoulder to check the canoe— still 50 yards away. Plenty of time to land the fish. I turned to focus on the fish, and to my shocked surprise, the osprey left his perch and glided over the water toward me, zeroing in on my thrashing fish. Within a second or two, the raptor extended his claws and crashed into the water. "Get out of here!" I yelled. He did, but not before slicing my tippet with his razor-sharp talons. The bird flew off without the trout and started circling back to the tree. My line went limp and the fish disappeared somewhere in the deep. Turning again toward the canoe, the craft was within ten yards of me.

"I've never seen anything like that before," the front paddler quipped.

"Yeah, me either," I shot back.

*   *   *   *   *   *   *

Tricorythodes, better known as tricos to fly anglers, are a tiny genus of mayfly of which sixteen species exist. I had never heard of tricos before I started fishing the Tulpehocken, and when a friendly angler showed me one on the end of his tippet, my first thought was, *oh my, this is almost as small as the period at the end of a sentence.* I may be exaggerating a bit, but these flies range in size from #18 in the west to #24 and #26 in the east, about the size of a common gnat. My transition from size #16 and #18 caddis to these tiny specimens required a shrinking of tippet size down to sizes 7X and 8X, truly entering the world of "technical" fishing. I managed to accomplish this type of fishing and, at the same time, become more adept at tying flies. I began to really like the trico hatch. It afforded me trout fishing opportunities in southeastern Pennsylvania in July when most trout anglers have moved on to bass and other warm water species. In that Golden Age of the Tulpehocken between 1985 to 1990 when the PA Fish and Boat Commission was stocking the stream exclusively with fingerlings, the fish lent themselves, as one fish warden I encountered described it, as "almost wild." They were not as skittish as wild fish, but the fins were beautifully intact and the fish strong and muscular. Anyone who had fished for stocked adult trout could tell the difference. And the phrase "almost wild" intrigued me. I knew the sunfish, bass, and catfish I grew up catching were all wild, but a wild trout was almost an alien species in southeastern Pennsylvania. Progress and civilization had all but guaranteed extermination of wild trout in that part of the state. In any case, fishing "almost wild" trout led trout led me to explore another facet of my fishing development: conservation. I'll go into detail later, but my chance purchase of a magazine called *Trout* at a local pharmacy gave me an opportunity to explore my wild side. I decided to reconstitute the lapsed chapter of Trout Unlimited in my own watershed, the Perkiomen Creek. Getting to that required my exhausting the fishing challenges on the Tully.

The weather leading up to July of 1990 proved to be fairly hot and dry. Usually that is fine for trico fishing as most of it occurs in the cool, early mornings, but it meant that the caddis hatches tailed off dramatically from mid-June onward. Nonetheless, I was looking forward to the Trico hatch on the Tully that year. The first day of the month fell on a Sunday, so I figured it would be an ideal day to visit the stream, hoping that at least some of my angling brethren had another religion besides fly-fishing. Unfortunately, that would not be the case. When I turned on to the pull-off to park, there was only one other car, so it looked like there would be sufficient room to roam. Ha. By the time I got to the back of my van, two more cars pulled in and their occupants, who must have slept in their waders, immediately hopped out and made their way to the stream. By the time I got my waders on and adjusted my gear, the lot was full. After making my way across Rebers Bridge and gliding the path to my desired streamside destination, there were anglers literally fifteen feet on either side of me. The hatch was mediocre at best. Worse yet, the fish were not moving at all. I had never seen this before. Not sure if all the gridlock on the banks caused the deficit in rises, but the fishing experience was akin to birdwatching at the Mummers Parade. Yeah, you'll see lots of feathers, but not any birds. I think I lasted a half-hour before packing it in. The hatch never really materialized and the jamboree on the banks forced me to accept what I did not want to believe: the Tully was becoming a victim of its own success. Like many other popular rivers, what was my dream stream had become the destination waters of southeastern Pennsylvania for hundreds and maybe thousands of regional anglers. It boasted a successful fly shop, Tulpehocken Creek Outfitters, that has become a regional player in the fly-fishing industry. The stream got featured in an article in *Fly Fisherman* magazine and the local Tulpehocken Chapter of Trout Unlimited eventually won the National Trout Unlimited Gold Trout Award in 1998. These are all good things in many respects for a trout stream, but if the most valued part of your fly-fishing experience is solitude, as it was becoming for me, then it was time for me to reluctantly move on.

5

The New World

May 1969

Police Dispatcher: Patrol 237, come in please.

Officer: This is 237 reading you.

Dispatcher: What's your status there? Do you need backup?

Officer: No backup needed.

Dispatcher: Is he out of the compound?

Officer: Affirmative.

Dispatcher: Forcible arrest?

Officer: No, he left on his own, with the county social worker.

Dispatcher: Any weapons?

Officer: No, he was unarmed. Took a bunch of fishing rods out with him though, maybe a dozen or more. And a duffel bag with some clothes and a box of pots and pans.

Dispatcher: What about the dogs? Did you see the dogs?

Officer: No, the dogs were gone when I got here. He probably let them go last night.

Dispatcher: Well, go look for the dogs and shoot them. I'll call you if I get any sightings. Over.

Officer: Over and out.

Officer Brad Dougherty drove his patrol car up the road to the first residence he encountered, a squat, two-story bungalow with moldy cedar shake siding flaking off the sides. Around back was Ray Burger, known to the kids in the village as Old Man Burger, a fellow of about sixty, both stocky and chubby, with a perpetual gruff affect. He stood peering past his apple trees across the gravel road where the county van was laden with the remaining effects that Indian Joe decided to take with him after his long standoff. Officer Dougherty lifted himself out of the patrol car and approached.

"Morning sir. Have you seen any loose dogs around here?"

"His dogs, you mean? The Shepherd/Malamute cross and the big, ugly, red mongrel?"

"Yeah, those dogs," Dougherty affirmed as he took on a more determined look.

"Wolf's the half-breed. Fox is the mongrel. They're dangerous. Are they out?" Burger queried.

"We think so."

"You'd better find them," Burger growled as he shook his head from side to side. "They're old and testy now but still fierce. Only he could control them, you know."

"Yeah, I've got orders to shoot them. Have you seen them?"

"No." Burger looked one way, then the other. The alarm in his eyes subsided enough to allow him to probe the officer. "This may be none of my business, but where are they taking him?"

"Probably to the psych ward in the hospital for observation first. Then up to the Poconos."

"Way up there? Why they doin' that?"

"It's where he requested the county buy him another property after they condemned that one."

"That's where you'll find the dogs then. They're loyal to him. You watch."

"From down here in Newportville? Hell, that's over 120 miles. They'll never get up that far. How they gonna pick up his scent?" Dougherty spit as he glared at Burger.

"They'll be there. You'll see. They're sly like he was."

"Well, if you see them, call us," Dougherty offered as he slid back into the patrol car.

July 1955

"Louie, where are you going?" my mother inquired.

"I'm going down the creek, Mom."

"Where?" she insisted.

"Down at The Steps."

"You be careful. You just learned to swim. And stay away from Indian Joe's. You know how vicious his dogs are. I don't like you going down there alone."

"I'll be okay. They can't get out."

"I hope not."

Wearing a sharp, blue bathing suit and carrying a small plastic bucket, I stomped down the gentle slope away from my house toward the Neshaminy Creek, the local stream of my boyhood, only a few hundred yards from our house. At the bottom of the slope, I swerved right on to the gravel road that led directly past Indian Joe's compound. As I approached the makeshift fence, thrown together from slats of weathered mill lumber washed down from previous floods, the dogs appeared, forcing low, grating growls as they pushed their wet, dirty noses through the fence. I edged over to the far side of the road as if the little bit of distance would offer better protection should the dogs escape. Walking softly past the length of the fence, I peered constantly over my left shoulder, staring intently through the overgrown thickets along the outside border of those slats, hoping to catch a glimpse of Indian Joe, who I never saw but had heard about many times. Instead, all I could see were faint features of the humble shack inside the enclosure, a one-story rustic affair cobbled together from the flotsam left by the creek's high waters. A flat, tarpaper roof covered the sturdy frame structure sided with faded, gray asbestos shingles and adorned by a few irregular windows with brown paint peeling off the trim at frequent intervals. At the end of the property, the fence turned sharply left toward the creek. Thick clusters of native willows mixed with silky dogwood shrouded my view. The dogs followed me around the perimeter, slick wet tongues drooping out of their mouths, eyes fixed on me like hardened steel daggers. Still, there was no sign of Indian Joe.

August 1955, a few days after the great flood.

Deke Hoffmeister fished with a passion, mostly for bottom fish: carp, catfish, and even eels. Almost all his fishing was done from the early evening into the night. He usually quit by ten, when the feeding slowed. He always fished downstream from Indian Joe's at The Steps, a set of gneiss shelves quarried and cut to the size of a large dining room table installed by Old Man Burger. Indian Joe never asked Deke to fish on his property, and there's some who think that he would never accept even if he was offered. He was, of course, Old Man Hoffmeister to the neighborhood kids, and at seventy he was truly ancient in their minds.

The flood from the remnants of Hurricane Diane was the worst in a hundred years—one of disastrous proportions—inundating the Neshaminy Valley with sloppy brown water and covering many houses right over their rooftops. All kinds of debris washed down the creek: boats ripped from their moorings, wooden windows, sides of houses, whole trees—everything imaginable that wasn't on higher ground. Myself and a couple of other neighborhood kids surveyed the damage—in awe of the brute strength of raging flood waters—when we followed Deke's station wagon down Fulton Road to Ray Burger's place. Silty, coffee-colored water lapped against the second-floor window as Ray Burger stood on the only rise on the edge of his property, about fifty yards from his house. Deke slid out of his old station wagon to offer consolation.

"Oh my, Ray, you've got a bad one there."

Ray stared at the soggy ground where grass blades lay limp as though drowned and lifeless. Without looking up at Deke, he wiped a tear from his eye.

"Look how high the water is. And it came on so fast, almost without warning. We lost a lot, maybe everything. I don't know how much the flood insurance will cover, but there's things you can't replace. You know—pictures, letters, important papers. I don't know…Ethel's with her sister. She can't bear to watch."

"There's not much you can do," Deke muttered, searching for a kind of solace to ease Ray's pain.

"Nah. Just clean up, rebuild, and go on as best you can."

"Yep," Deke affirmed. He looked farther down the road and motioned with his thick fingers. "Jeez, looks like Indian Joe's place is gone. I can't see anything, and the water's really hurryin' through there."

Ray lifted his eyes toward the spot where Indian Joe's shanty should have been, studying the swaying motion of the large trees that surrounded the shack with chocolate, debris-filled water wrapping around the dense trunks up past the first large limbs.

"I've not seen him since the water started risin'. He had the dogs on a thick rope, heading up the road with a duffel bag over his shoulder. Not sure where he went. He doesn't have any people around here that I know of."

"Well, I'm sure he's washed out now," Deke offered.

"Don't you bet on it. I know him. He'll be here when the water goes down. Won't say anything to anybody, just clean up and go on. This is not his first flood, not living on the creek like that. He's been around here longer than all of us."

We boys scattered as Deke quickly turned back toward his car. These were solemn times. No one had much to say as we walked back up the hill. Floods are a creek's mastery of those who try to hem them in with houses and shacks. These were lessons learned early in the lives of young boys whose houses were safely situated on high ground. This may have been our first flood, but you never expected it to be anybody's last.

September 1955, two weeks after the great flood.

A few friends and I went down to the creek to survey the post-flood conditions after receiving typhoid shots from the county health department. The flood water receded, yet the banks were slick with a slippery coating that smelled primeval, as if the earth were transformed to its prehistoric beginnings. While we were there, Deke showed up for his own reconnaissance mission, checking to see if the stream was fit to fish. The Steps were coated with the muddy slime, though the water was now only slightly silty, like it might be after an all-night spring rain. He retreated to Fulton Road where he stopped to see Ray, who was raking the mud off his front steps. We boys followed behind, careful to let the adults do the talking.

"How's it goin', Ray?"

"It's goin'. Been down to the creek yet?"

"Yeah, don't look too bad. If that awful mud dries, I might go fishin' tomorrow."

"You see what Indian Joe did?" Burger queried.

"No. I can't imagine there's anything thing he could do. Did he lose everything?"

"Go up on the berm and look over the fence."

Deke paced a short distance to the edge of Ray's property. Arching a glance over the fence, he gazed with a mixture of astonishment and curiosity at Indian's Joe's shack. Not only was it still intact but anointed on the top was a sharply pointed steeple like you might find at the top of a small chapel. Dried mud, apparently recently wiped off, matted around the perimeter of the shack. Atop the steeple, pointing towards the sky, was a weathervane decorated at its center with the silhouette of a gamefish, perhaps a pike. Deke closed over to Ray. "Jeezus, when did he do that?"

"Right after the water receded. I guess the steeple washed up on his property, and somehow he got it up there, with pulleys and hoists most likely."

"No damage to the cabin other than water and mud?"

"I guess so," Ray bristled.

"How's the fence? Can he keep the dogs in?"

"Apparently. No one's seen them since the flood, but I guess they're in there with him."

May 1958

A few of my angling buddies and I eagerly awaited the white bass run every spring along the Neshaminy. Other fish were available—sunnies, smallmouth, catfish—but the white bass came up from the Delaware estuary, forty miles downstream, for their spawning run. On this day, we cautiously skirted Indian Joe's, pausing before approaching The Steps, where we intended to set up our rods after turning over a few rocks to find worms, grubs, or salamanders to use as bait. About the time our bait was gathered we heard a gruff call directed our way.

"Hey, you kids want to fish over here?"

We looked at each other, somewhat in disbelief. It was Indian Joe. We had heard of a few folks being invited to fish behind his place, mostly the Whyte brothers from Fernwood Road. Some thought that they might be Indian or have Indian blood; Harry Whyte's older brother had unmistakable features: high cheek bones; long, shiny, jet-black hair, and a certain build that was hard to describe, but he carried himself with a kind of posture cloaked in mystery. Of course, nobody admitted to anything.

"Come over. I won't hurt you."

We could see him now, his chin tucked between the slats in the makeshift fence, wearing what looked to be an olive drab Army fatigue cap.

"We're afraid of the dogs!" I yelled back.

"They won't hurt you. I'll keep them behind the gate."

I looked at my friends Ronnie and Gerry. With his eyes and a slight head gesture, Gerry motioned to go ahead. I, too, thought it might be a good idea. Everybody heard that the fishing was better at Indian Joe's. We wanted to give it a try. The three of us moved forward cautiously, our rods swinging against the thick bushes near the creek's edge. At the back of Joe's property, the creek passed beside a stone embankment that Joe built by pulling rocks out of the channel, deepening the creek for a better sanctuary for fish in the process.

We set up our lines and fished while Joe looked on silently, occasionally puffing a corncob pipe. Joe kept his promise, keeping the distrustful dogs behind the weathered wooden gate, though I fished with one eye on my line and my ears cocked for any unusual movements the dogs might make. We stayed for the remainder of the morning, until the sun was high, fishing intently without any cross conversation. We were too afraid to say much, and Joe was content to watch. We did find the rumors to be true. The fishing was better at Indian Joe's. We gave him our catch and when the fishing got slow, we told Joe we had to be home for lunch. The dogs never once bothered us, but they did follow us along the whole length of the fence, poking their wet noses through the slats occasionally and offering low growls. On the road back to our homes, far enough so that Joe wouldn't hear, we bantered excitedly.

"He didn't seem so bad to me," I blurted.

"He didn't look like an Indian. I thought they had black hair," Gerry protested.

"Well, he could be an old Indian. They're gray, you know. I saw one on TV who was all gray!" I countered.

"Yeah, but what about that stubble?" Ronnie interjected, referring to Joe looking two days away from his last shave.

"Well, nobody said he was *full* Indian. He could be *half* Indian. That counts too," I refuted. "And I know one thing for sure—those are Indian dogs," I asserted as if some kind of expert "Wolf and Fox…they gotta be Indian dogs."

"Yep," Ronnie agreed. We both looked at Gerry for confirmation.

"Yep, no doubt about it," Gerry opined. "And he's the only one who could handle them. Did you see the way they held their heads down when he yelled at them? Only an Indian could do that. Yep, they're all Indian."

We boys lurched smugly up the hill away from the creek, reasoning that we possessed secret knowledge.

July 1960

At thirteen years old, I always considered it a real privilege to be invited over to Indian Joe's to fish. I didn't get invited often, only when Indian Joe—by some unpredictable quirk— relented and asked me and my friends to come over. This particular evening, I went down to the creek alone, after the afternoon swimmers had left the pool by The Steps. As I walked by Joe's compound, I saw no sign of the dogs. This could only mean one thing—that Indian Joe was in the back of his place fishing by himself and his dogs were laying there with him. Joe caught all kinds of fish from his bank: carp, sunnies, catfish, eels, bass, or whatever took his bait of worms and grubs. He usually cleaned them right on the bank and fed the heads and guts to the dogs. They ate fish too, though they didn't seem as keen on them as Joe. I guessed that he probably didn't feed them anything else, so if they didn't eat fish, they'd starve. I've often marveled at the smartness of dogs.

As I headed for The Steps, I heard a raspy call. Joe never called any of us kids by name. He probably didn't want to be bothered with remembering names.

"Hey kid." A short pause of silence intervened until Joe was certain I had heard the call. "You want to come over here and fish?" I hesitated. I had never been over there alone.

"Uh… okay."

I made my way through the narrow path, thick with short, snappy native willows on creek side and jewelweed mixed with nasty nettle on the other that led to the back of Indian Joe's property. It was a gauntlet of sorts, in which a rod always had a chance of snagging a branch. The bank dropped off steeply down to the slack water where water snakes and snapping turtles often floated motionless in search of prey. Behind the property, where his back gate led to his steeple-topped shanty, there was a small clearing with enough room for three or four people to fish comfortably. Shoeless, dressed in a sleeveless, stained T-shirt and blue denim cut-off shorts, Indian Joe was sitting on a three-legged stool, Fox at his side, while Wolf lay farther up by the gate. The dogs let off a low growl as I approached until Joe hushed them. He had two rods in the water, and a half-finished quart of beer sat on the grass near the edge of his stool.

"Any luck?" I nervously inquired.

"Nah. Just got started."

I baited up and sent a cast screaming out to the middle of the creek, then sat on a rock near the water.

"Nice cast, kid. Did your folks buy you that rod?"

I looked down at my department store spinning outfit and then over at Joe's equipment. A beat-up bait caster lay near Joe's feet, line lying limp as it trailed off into the water. A split-cane deep-sea rig perched on a basketball-sized rock, thick and stocky, with a braided, white nylon line stretched tautly in to the current. This was his big fish line I figured, the one that he'd use to horse in a big carp or channel cat, should he be so lucky.

"Yeah."

"How much did it cost?"

"I don't know, maybe ten bucks," I answered bashfully.

"It's a nice rod, kid. Don't leave it lying around or somebody'll take it."

"No. No, I won't do that. I love fishin' too much."

"Me too, kid. I eat 'em all, too."

"I know. I'll give you mine if I catch any."

"That's good, kid," Joe uttered in a gravelly voice.

I sat there watching my line. There was a long, uncomfortable silence. The fish weren't biting. I fished cautiously, my ear attuned for any sudden movement of the dogs. Joe took a swig of beer from the bottle every so often. Just then, Fox got up and started for me.

"He won't hurt you, just don't make any sudden moves."

Frozen like a granite statue, I let the rust-colored mongrel sniff me around the ears and face. When it looked like he was annoying me, Joe called him back over to his side. Another long silence. Still no fish were biting. It was a bad evening, even at Indian Joe's.

"Hey kid, have you put your weenie in a girl yet?" Joe moaned in a low guttural heave, chuckling in such a way that his rolled eyes and the near-empty bottle suggested that it had been a long time since he had done anything with his. I quickly glanced at Indian Joe, then back out at the water. I didn't know how to respond to such a ridiculous, curious question. No one had ever asked me anything like that before.

"Na…look, you're getting a bite!" I shouted excitedly, pointing at Joe's line.

"All right, all right. Quiet or you'll scare the fish," Joe ordered as he crept closer to the jerking line of the bait-caster. Joe studied the line, waiting for the right time to strike, the time in fishing when conversation ends and concentration rules. I barely breathed, though I did silently thank God that the fishing was always good at Indian Joe's.

December 1961

"Alan," I called, "don't go out so far!"

Alan ignored my admonition. Sliding his feet apart, inching farther out over the newly formed shelf ice that extended beyond the older, firmer ice in the slack water, Alan ventured toward the center of the creek where the current moved slightly faster, the ice thinner. He offered a wry smile when looking back at me as if to flaunt his courage. I stayed on the thicker ledge ice, wondering if Alan would foolishly try to make it to the opposite bank.

"Come on out, it's okay," Alan urged.

"It's thinner…"

Before I could finish, the ice beneath Alan cracked sharply at once, then he dropped straight down into the frigid water. He quickly spread his arms and caught the edge of the hole, his arms and head above water, the rest of him dangling helplessly in the frigid syrup.

"Alan! Get up! Get out of there!" I cried.

"I can't!"

Each time Alan tried to hoist himself on the ice, more of it would break loose, widening the hole. He started to panic, flailing harder to pull himself out, only to dislodge more thin ice around the hole.

"Help me, Louie," Alan pleaded. "I'm freezing. I'm scared!"

I stood there, immobilized. I knew I couldn't venture out there, or I myself would slip through the ice and maybe drown as I feared my friend Alan might.

"HELP!"

"HELP HELP HELP HELP!" I started screaming, terrified of what was happening, knowing that I couldn't help Alan, knowing that Alan was weakening, his face smothered in a ghastly fear I had never seen before in anyone. I turned and started to run to the road for help.

"What's the matter, kid?" Indian Joe barked from inside his fence. I could barely see his face, desperation binding my lungs.

"My friend Alan is drowning. He fell through the ice. Help me! Help us!"

"I'll be right there. Go back and keep talking to him."

I obeyed, going back to Alan, coaching him to stay afloat. Alan's face started turning pale, his voice weak. He coughed water and stared blankly. As I looked back over my shoulder, I spied Indian Joe running along the bank with a long, battered, wood plank.

"Hold on to my feet," Joe instructed as he dropped to the ice on his stomach, the plank thrust out ahead of him toward Alan. The plank was three feet short.

"You lay down too. Hook your feet on the rocks."

I did as I was told while holding Joe's ankles as he inched out to the thinner ice, shoving the board to the edge of the hole where Alan, tears streaming down his shivering face, barely had the strength to continue.

"Grab the board, kid," Joe ordered. Alan reached with his right arm, barely grasping the plank, his wet glove resting on his only link to safety.

"Now pull yourself up. We can't go out any farther. You have to save yourself now."

Alan nodded faintly, put his other hand on the plank, and began wiggling his hips out of the water, his heavy, water-laden boots slashing the ice behind him. Eventually he slid out of the hole, like a seal in the Arctic, his clothes dripping on the thin layer of ice supporting his exhausted body. Alan pulled and shimmied along the board until he reached Indian Joe. Both of them inched back to the bank before standing up.

"Come on over to my place. I've got a good fire in the wood stove." The three of us trudged over to Indian Joe's compound. Alan's chattering teeth cast the sound of intense suffering and pain. We made our way inside the shack.

Alan stared at the ceiling, not wanting to make eye contact with either myself or Joe, ashamed of his foolishness. Instead, he stared at the off-white plaster, dingy with water stains, buckles, and cracks, much like the ice that gave way earlier. He moved his gaze over to the cast iron stove. A few seasoned skillets hung over the stove, but nothing else adorned the small room. Through a doorway, a limp two-cushion couch, stale and decrepit, rested on the floor. Patches of scuffed linoleum, curled at the edges, spread about the floor in an array of chaotic patterns. It was the first glimpse either of us ever had of the inside of Joe's shack. Compared to the houses we lived in, it was, to be kind, humble.

Joe brought a dim-yellow blanket from another room, a bedroom I guessed, and tossed it over to Alan. For what seemed like a long time, he sat impassively with the blanket wrapped around him. Just now remembering the dogs, I scanned the room carefully but did not see them anywhere even though two bowls and a water dish lay close to the stove. Joe stood up abruptly and moved toward the door.

"Take the blanket with you and go home," he instructed, nodding to Alan, "and get out of those wet clothes as soon as possible. And don't be so asinine again."

Alan offered a sheepish smile, and we were grateful that everything would be okay.

August 1963

I took my rod down to The Steps one evening to try my luck on this hot, humid evening. Upstream, Indian Joe appeared busy with some kind of construction project on the far end of his property. After only a few minutes, I heard some conversation behind me. It was Deke and Ray Burger. Old Man Burger rarely went down to the creek in the evenings. He didn't fish, and Deke never tried to coax him into it, seeming to prefer to fish alone, perhaps to distance himself from troubles and people, looking to fishing to soothe those kinds of irritations in some sort of meaningful way. Even at a young age, I understood the psychology of fishing. I was engaged in it myself. Home life could be abrasive at times. Young boys should not have to endure it. I guessed that Deke never thought about anything except catching fish when his lines were in the water—he was a lot like Indian Joe in that regard. This evening though, Old Man Burger flagged him down before he got to the water, and both of them followed the path down to The Steps. Burger focused neither on the water nor fishing, so when they got to the bank he came to an abrupt halt, turned to his left, and just pointed upstream. I swiveled my gaze upstream as well as the old men talked.

"My God, what is he doing now?" Deke mumbled.

"He's protecting his investment, that's what."

"How?"

"By building that big jetty on the edge of his property where it meets the creek to try to deter those awful flood waters from washing away that shanty of his."

"Hell, the floods'll take it someday, you watch."

"Nah," Old Man Burger shook his head, "he'll die there, come Hell or high water."

Deke laughed snidely as he watched Indian Joe pile rocks from the creek bottom on to a handmade platform suspended from a pulley attached to a thick cable strung for some hundred yards from the corner of his property to a tall, mature sycamore on the opposite bank. The rocks—most the size of footballs—were hauled up to the bank where they were heaped against his fence in an effort to create a massive piling that would divert the creek away from his hut. In the process, he made the tail of the rapids deeper, offering even better holding water for fish than was directly behind his property. Apparently, he had been at it for two weeks before Old Man Burger discovered what was going on.

"Think they'll say anything to him?" Deke challenged.

"Who's they? The police? The township? Nobody ever comes around here. Besides, what's he hurtin'? Ain't that gonna be better fishing?"

"Yeah, I guess you're right. And that part of the creek ain't his, so I can go there if I want." Deke looked about as if he was sizing up his prospects for the evening.

"I'd watch out for those dogs though. They don't know nothin' about property lines," Burger offered as he turned to go back to his house. "Good luck fishing tonight. And don't let the kid here out-fish you tonight," he snickered, nodding toward me. I smiled to myself when he said that but stared straight ahead as if inattentive to their conversations and folk wisdom.

June 1965

Butchie Burger, the grandson of Ray Burger, lived in Clearfield in central Pennsylvania, an old coal mining town about forty miles northwest of State College. I befriended him on his visits to his grandfather's house where he visited every summer. We got to be pretty good friends, often fishing and swimming together in the creek. Both being recently graduated high school seniors, we decided to meet down by The Steps for a little evening fishing, our last time spent together as it turned out. As we proceeded to The Steps, the old, wooden screen door at Indian Joe's slammed against the frame of the shack several times, letting we boys know he was stirring about, and the dogs were probably loose. We fished, hoping we wouldn't attract the attention of Wolf and Fox who frequently crept away from their compound when Joe was occupied with one of his property improvement projects. Keeping a low profile was always the smart thing to do in those situations. With little commotion, we readied and cast our lines.

"So, Louie, what are you going to do after graduation?" Butchie whispered as he let his bobber drift in the slow eddy in from the main current.

"I'll probably go to college."

"Really? What would you do there?"

"Study."

"I know that," Butchie snarled impatiently. "What would you study?"

"I don't know. I never thought about it. It's just what you do in college. You study everything then settle on one thing that makes your boot heels click."

"Why don't you study about Indians?"

"Indians? What are you, crazy? You can't make any money doing that!"

"I wasn't talking about money. I was thinking about history. Look around you. See this place, it's changed since the first settlers. There were lots of Indians here at one time. Now they're gone. Where did they go? That's one thing you could look into at college." Butchie stared ahead as his bobber danced softly, the evening glare smearing the water like hot, melted butter. I felt challenged by Butchie, not in an unfriendly way, just moved off-center, as I hadn't given any thought to my future, or history, or Indians, or much of anything. I was just graduating from high school, and that was enough for now.

"You know, Butchie, things are never going to be the same, even around here. Look at Indian Joe over there. He's probably the last Indian around this whole area," I said, motioning with my arms as if to set off a vast, definable expanse like the mythical Ponderosa or the Badlands. "And I don't know if anybody gives a flyin' damn. So, what would be the point in studying about that, about Indians and stuff?"

"Well," Butchie stammered, "I just thought it would be interesting. Besides, you said you didn't know what you wanted to study, and I was just giving you ideas."

"Well, I can't make you any promises. Maybe I just might, or maybe you should do it."

"But I'm not going to college. I'm moving out of that crummy old coal town and getting a job," Butchie insisted.

We fished intently for a long time, the occasional splashes of a feeding bass breaking the silence. The sun squeezed between the trees before disappearing. Amber fringe hung in the sky above, the new sky of summer that summons fresh raspberries and idle fishing. Nightfall was approaching. I motioned with my hand in Butchie's direction to get his attention.

"Last cast," I whispered while whipping my rod sharply. The whirl of the nylon spool sizzled across the creek, then the C.P. Swing slashed the water sharply. I reeled the lure back to the bank.

"We ought to be quiet. If Joe's dogs are out, we could be stuck here for a long time," Butchie chirped back. We reeled in our lines and vague recollections as we slipped silently past Indian Joe's compound into the near darkness.

*   *   *   *   *   *   *

The Neshaminy Creek still calls me when I am alone, letting my mind drift back to my boyhood. I hadn't fished there in more than thirty years, but a recent visit revealed that hardly anybody goes down to that place anymore, and those that do have no idea how it was before. Oh, occasionally there may be few idle fishers but not any passionate disciples. The stout sycamores and sweeping maples remain, though the ledge rock that formed The Steps where we sat with crude fishing rods is overgrown with brush right down to the stream's edge. Little of Indian Joe's scant legacy is revealed, so memory serves as a kind of history in the filaments of the subconscious. Only native shrubs surround that old property. The steeple-topped shanty is gone, obliterated by notions of progress. All that's left is a strange pile of boulders that defy the creek when the turbid waters run high and bold.

Every now and then, I get up to the Poconos to fly fish the freestone streams. Before each trip, I usually scan a topo map to choose a stream or river, perhaps to accidentally discover an unmolested section of stream for some memorable fishing. The names roll and twist off my tongue, the syllables bumping into each other like strangers at a crowded carnival... the Aquishicola, Mauch Chunk, Quakake, the Nesquehoning, Tobyhanna, Wallenpaupack. The names are the only remnants of a once-thriving native culture connected more closely with the natural and spirit world than our own. Now they are geographical features harboring trout, primarily European browns, descendants of the same continent as most of the fly fishers who seek them for leisure sport.

The Lackawanna holds wild trout again and even has a Trophy Trout section. It's not a pretty stream where it winds past old mining towns, though it's made a remarkable recovery from the Age of Coal. The Lechauweeki, better known by the Pennsylvania German name, Lehigh, is a big, brawling river that features rafters who grit their teeth at approaching whitewater. It gets yearly plants of hatchery trout, some of which eventually attain considerable size. My favorite stream, though, is the Pohopoco near Kresgeville. Silky dogwoods compete with native willows to choke its banks as the stream twists through second-growth forest and overgrown pastures almost hidden from the casual passerby. I've taken some respectable wild browns that sip blue-winged olives in the long, smooth glides between riffles. They spook easily, so you must be quiet and careful. It's an eerie, almost haunting place back in those moist woodland bogs where the stream quietly meanders. A hard place to get to, you'll recognize it when you're there though. You have to fish it with one eye on your line and your ear cocked for rustling in the bushes. Don't be alarmed at the pacing and panting of suspicious dogs. Stare them down with a mean and dirty look and sternly scold them.

"Quiet, Wolf! Quiet, Fox!"

Then whisper...

"Where's Joe?"

6

Demons

Father (to his twelve-year-old son): Get out of bed. You're going to work with me this morning.

Son: But it's Saturday, and I was going to play football with my friends today.

Father: It's time to grow up and forget that kid's stuff. You need to find out what working for a living is all about.

Son: Ah, do I have to?

Father: Yeah, goddamit. Now get up. I don't want to have to warn you again.

+   +   +   +   +   +   +   +

Father: Get in to one of the professions. Doctors, lawyers, dentists... they make good money, easy money. Be a dentist. You could do that.

Son: Uh huh. *But I want to be a weatherman.*

+   +   +   +   +   +   +   +

Father (exhorting): You gotta have moxie! My father never had it. That's why he was always poor.

Son: Uh huh. *What's he talking about now?*

Father: You gotta take chances. Get it?

Son: Yep. I got it. *Phew, anything to shut him up.*

+   +   +   +   +   +   +   +

Father (demonstratively): You wanna know how to get ahead?

Son: (meekly) How? *Actually, I wasn't thinking about that.*

Father (in a passionately angry tone): You have to have desire! And sacrifice! You have to sacrifice. That's how you get ahead in life! I worked hard for everything I got. Nobody ever gave me anything.

Son: Oh. *Not me, either.*

*   *   *   *   *   *   *

Nobody thinks "trout streams" when they think of Philadelphia. Yes, there are historical references to brook trout being caught in the Schuylkill River (1789 in the tidal section below the Fairmont Water Works), but the thick virgin forests were decimated, dams were built, and the fishery was extirpated in a short period of time. Now there are hatchery planted trout in Penn's "greene Country Towne" in the park spaces where the Pennypack and Wissahickon Creeks flow. These trout are quickly removed by neighborhood locals as their life expectancy is measured in days and weeks, not months or years. West of the city of

Philadelphia, Valley Creek winds through a greenspace that includes the historic Valley Forge National Park before it empties into the Schuylkill River. The park encompasses 3,500 acres as a national monument to the troops of the Continental Army who encamped here in the winter of 1777-78. Yes, Washington slept here, though not in one of the 2,000 huts constructed in city-block fashion across a vast acreage, but rather in the farmhouse of the local miller Isaac Potts. The creek, on the western edge of the park, parallels Route 252 along the lower half of its journey to the river. Today it harbors wild, brown trout, some as large as 18 inches, as it flows north from its source in a narrow, protective riparian buffer surrounded by densely populated suburbs. It offers a refuge to ardent anglers who seek a difficult quarry in heavily fished public lands.

A small stream about fifteen to twenty-five feet wide that flows through a limestone belt, Valley Creek contains numerous underground springs cooling the water even on the hottest summer days. In one of the ironies of fisheries management, pollution has been responsible for an enhanced fishery. It seems that the former Pennsylvania Railroad was responsible for polluting the creek by allowing PCBs (polychlorinated biphenyls) to leak from transformers. By the time the railroad emerged from bankruptcy into Conrail, the Pennsylvania Fish Commission stopped stocking the stream after the discovery of the cancer-causing chemicals. The fish, which store the PCBs in their fat, were otherwise unaffected. A few wild trout multiplied into many, and Valley Creek became the best wild trout fishery in southeast Pennsylvania, which is saying something when you consider that Philadelphia's city limit is less than fifteen minutes away, and the country's second-largest mall only five. Essentially, it's a Class-A water full of inedible fish. The Valley Forge Chapter of Trout Unlimited stewards this stream and other Chester County trout fisheries exceptionally well, given the challenges at hand. Though it has pressed Conrail and subsequent ownership to clean up, there's a part of me that thinks that PCBs might be an effective deterrent to overfishing. Sometimes I'm half-tempted to make up warning signs and post along other streams.

Unlike some of the trout bums that we'd all love to emulate, I grind hard for a living, and one particular Saturday in June at the end of a six-day work week, I couldn't get on the water until around four-thirty in the afternoon. Since Valley Creek was only a half hour from my house, I decided to take a run over there to finish out the evening by working over some chemically enhanced wild fish. It was the quickest stress anecdote I could muster, other than pulling into a local bar. Besides, I hadn't fished in a week and I was beginning to have slurred speech, shaking hands, and other symptoms that addicts get when their fix is running low. I pulled into a parking area in the middle section of the stream near the covered bridge on Route 252 and quickly opened the rear hatch of my van, when I was immediately confronted by two National Park Service rangers looking me over suspiciously.

"Did you just get here?" one of them asks.

"Yeah."

The other looks over my waders and rod tube and asks the obvious.

"Did you come here to fish?"

"Yeah, why, is there something wrong?"

"We've gotten reports that a guy dressed in fatigues carrying an assault rifle is making menacing threats to passers-by. He was last seen on that hill above the creek. You haven't seen anybody like that, have you?"

"No."

The first ranger then steps forward, sweeps his gaze in both directions, and offers a sobering warning.

"We're asking people not to use the park until we've got this situation under control. We can't order you to leave, we just think it'd be safer for right now."

My immediate reaction was thoughtful and deliberate. Hell, I'm not crazy. I'm not going to risk getting myself killed for a little stint on a stream.

"Thank you, gentleman. I think I'm leaving."

I started back down the highway. As I crossed that covered bridge, I looked longingly toward the water sluicing through the small gorge cut into the rocky slopes. Suddenly my mood changed. A growing resentment overcame me. I mean, I worked all goddam week for a few hours of solitary pleasure on a trout stream only to have a disturbed, gun-toting wingnut take it away? Not today, honey. I slid the van into the next pull-off, a half-mile down the road. There I donned my waders defiantly, threw on my vest, and strode over the guard-rail down to the stream. It was a section of water I had not fished, about twenty feet across at the widest point. I crossed the stream twenty yards below to circle around to the head of a long, narrow pool. I felt proud and foolishly brave for having stood up to that unseen evil. It was time to fish.

A large beech dropped its lower branches over the deepest part of the pool, offering shade and protection. It looked promising. I lowered to my haunches and searched for my fly box. A small caddis was a likely choice, and I tied on a #20 deer hair. As I was doing so, dimples started to appear underneath the low-hanging branches. There was only about a foot and a half of clearance between the water's surface and the lowest branch, calling for an accurate and delicate sidearm cast. The bushes behind me crowded my backcast. My first cast snagged a stem of tall grass behind me. Frustrated, I crept back carefully to retrieve the fly, trying not to put down the only rising fish in the pool. I positioned myself again and sent a perfect cast over the fish. No inspection. Ten more casts between other rises yielded the same result. Wrong fly, I surmised. I studied the rise again more carefully. Blue-winged olive, of course. I dropped down to 8X tippet, thinking that the slow glide gave the fish plenty of time to scrutinize. After setting up, I knelt at the edge of the water. The sun descended behind the hillside, causing a slight chill in the still evening air. I prepared to cast. Then I heard the discernible rustle of crisp leaves. Snap! A dead branch behind me cracked sharply. Not wanting to turn around, I cringed in frozen stark terror, then silently prayed. *Please lord of tender mercies, I don't want to die. Not now. Not yet.*

7

Catskill Remembrances

The Schoharie is the poor stepsister of Catskill Rivers. Even though it flows through some of the loveliest country in the region, it is only marginal habitat for trout, especially below its confluence with the West Kill near the village of Lexington. Although Art Flick composed his streamside guide there, the times I've fished it have produced few memorable hatches and many disappointments. Where the stream meets the Westkill, it is stocked by the state as very few wild fish can survive the sun's unforgiving rays. There, the riparian buffer is markedly absent. Shade is desperately needed as warming waters deny trout the kind of temperatures that protective overhead offers on eastern streams. During my annual reunions in the Catskills each spring, I usually manage to make at least one trip over to the Schoharie. It's not so much a fishing outing as it is a pilgrimage, a chance to embrace the contributions Art Flick gave to our sport and the stream itself. His is truly a "bloom-where-you're-planted" story, and what I feel when I'm on this stream is a reverence not felt in other places in the Catskills, even the Beaverkill or Willowemoc. Those streams are steeped in a lot more tradition and have much better fishing, but the Schoharie to me represents one man's pursuit of trout and fly-fishing shaped by the flow of the river and the character of the man. It becomes more defined for me as I gaze down into the dairy valleys as the river winds its fated course. I envision a man who fished each pocket, pool, and riffle, carefully noting every emergence during the whims and vagaries of a brief, but cherished spring. I imagine a man who loved a stream that was ignored by most and probably scorned by a few.

There use to be a small group of fly-fishermen who planted willow trees along the banks of the Schoharie to continue an undertaking first started by Art Flick to improve his beloved water. Their doing that not only helped the stream, but more importantly kept his spirit alive. I've never fished with Art Flick, but I've stood under his willows many times, which I guess means I've fished with Art Flick.

*   *   *   *   *   *   *

The coastal plain along the southeastern edge of Pennsylvania bores me. Though there may be a variety of flora on close inspection, the lack of contour in the landscape easily dulls the senses and closes the imagination. The absence of rock outcroppings and even minor elevations discourages views, leaving the scenery with no discernible landmarks. The only area of the coastal plain that I have any interest in is the New Jersey coastline, where the land meets bays and estuaries which eventually salute the expansive Atlantic. The changing ecosystem there engenders a variety of bird and animal species that can hold your attention whether you're fishing, bird watching, or just snooping around.

As a flatlander, I've always been enamored with mountains. A land with changing contours suggests variety and invites the vistas that afford distinguishable landmarks and, in some cases, spectacular views. Hills and mountains freshen the air and broadcast the seasons with their expressive sheath of native trees; they provide opportunity for mystery and discovery. The landscape always begs questions: What is beyond the next bend? Is there a beckoning view? How does the hidden stream carve its way through the creases and folds of the mountains? Is there a bend-pool full of wild, skittish fish? When you are walking an expanse of contoured land, each turn seems to surprise with a new plant species configured upon the rugged forest floor— perhaps a stand of black birches holding a hillside from falling into a stream, or an array of flowering mountain laurel hiding a clump of wild blueberries is just beyond your view. It's easier to seize upon some wild creature poised in a tree or crossing the trail in search of prey or a safe haven. Walking itself is on trial. Rock and boulders dictate the rough texture here, confining travel to the path of least opposition. The mountains of Pennsylvania are among the smallest in the Appalachian Range. A look on any topographical map of the state reveals elevations seldom over 2,500 feet, and most of these occur in Laurel Highlands near Altoona. The Pocono region barely measures 2,000 feet, with many long plateaus and far fewer of the ridge and valley sequences so common in the central part of the state. Nonetheless, their intrigue has held me since I first encountered them while vacationing in the Pine Creek watershed with a neighboring family. My first introduction to wild trout occurred on this trip. The largest of the brookies barely extended past the palm of my outstretched hand after I hoisted them from an icy, clear mountain tributary. These brilliant trout looked hand-painted, as if pieces of glazed, ceramic figurines. The desperate little creatures were guiled by pink, squirmy worms dropped into the deeper pools. A nine-year-old boy has been romanced forever on the allure of trout fishing by this secret mountain brook, yielding a treasure that has been paying dividends ever since.

You might think that trips to the Rockies and Alaska would diminish my affection for the mountains of the east, but they haven't in the least. Our western mountains seem to project straight to the heavens. They appear more foreboding than inviting to me, causing me to feel dwarfed and inconsequential. The views are staggering, and their magnificence is undeniable, but they seem almost unapproachable. A day's hike barely reveals all the hidden splendor of these great peaks. I feel I've missed more than I've actually experienced when making off-road jaunts through the vast, scabrous terrain, and this is always confirmed when I watch nature programs on my local cable channel. I never seem to be able to come upon the dramas of wildlife that a camera, sometimes stationed for weeks or months, so easily brings into view. The eastern mountains appeal to me because they are, for the most part, more accessible; you could hike to the top of most of them in a few hours. They seem more reassuring, more engaging, and easier to embrace. Some appear as one long sweeping ridge, like Blue Mountain—named for the bluish tint it suggests when viewed at a distance from the Piedmont— which hoists the Appalachian Trail upon its back and provides the frontal mountainous boundary across almost all of Pennsylvania for those traveling from the east. Compared to the mountains of Pennsylvania though, the Catskills are far more enchanting. The peaks are much higher, the ruggedness of the contours more distinct, offering a flair of excitement as you approach them from almost any direction. They seem to arise from nowhere and assert themselves at once as a formidable barrier to further encroachment. Only when you realize that the way in is through the valleys of the Catskill rivers do you gain a degree of assurance that they can be easily traversed. My favorite entrance to these mountains is from the southwest, up the Neversink Valley from Woodbourne to Claryville, along the West Branch of the Neversink past Frost Valley toward Big Indian. An aura of ravishing barrenness seems to imbue the slopes and ridges, particularly in the early spring before the leaves fully form on the outstretched limbs of birches and oaks clinging on the steep inclines stretching to the summits. Their lure is an inexplicable stationary charisma that provokes my imagination. They may plea for exploration, as John Burroughs was beckoned more than 100 years earlier, though many times you'll settle for reverent adoration from a secure foothold next to a timeworn foundation of an earlier inhabitant's stone wall.

*   *   *   *   *   *   *

I clearly recall the first time I ever fished a Catskill stream. The smooth, hassock-sized boulders bordering the banks of the Esopus were scoured in the early spring from snowmelt, and a saturation of groundwater at the headwaters above Big Indian created chutes of whitewater tumbling toward the valley in April, when the fishing season first emerges. The crush of the icy, turbid water against the rocks echoed for hundreds of yards beyond the stream itself, offering a seduction long before I reached the stubble-strewn flanks of this determined little river. A group of us were stationed in housekeeping cottages in a meadow not far from the stream, deciding to meet in the Catskills when the course of our lives scattered our families beyond the jobs where we first came to know each other. For myself and many of the others, it was a first foray into these inviting surroundings. We were looking for a reunion escape within a few hour's drive of our present homes, and everyone agreed that an April weekend in the Catskills would be ideal. Our cabin was beyond rustic, a structure precariously balanced on rock pilings, two of which were close enough to the water to be in peril of being undercut by the forceful stream. My guess was that one good spate would have lifted the structure off its moorings and washed it right down the middle of the stream. We were located south of Big Indian along Oliverea Road where the headwaters of the Esopus literally slide off of Slide Mountain.

Aside from the condition of the cabin, it was probably a perfect introduction to the magic of the Catskills.

One evening I decided to give these headwaters a try. I hadn't brought my own rods for this trip, as it was more of a reunion amongst old friends, but my friend Bob brought an old 1950s-style Fiberglass rod with an auto-retracting reel as a "just-in-case" with a nondescript size #12 nymph tied to thick tippet at the end. The Esopus on this stretch during that spring was a bounding, rattling, gurgling chute of excitable water about fifteen feet wide, and I couldn't wait to give it a whirl. Escaping out the back of the cabin with Bob's gear, I surveyed the terrain and decided to push downstream where the stream bends at a sharp angle to the left. Every few yards, there was enough outcropping of rock to allow me room to cast, if I could squeeze both my sneakers on to a smooth boulder long enough to balance myself. Initially the rod felt awkward. It was like casting a telephone pole compared to the graphite rods I was used to. I waved the heavy wand back and forth several times, sloppily letting out line with each succeeding stroke of the rod. The first cast dropped with a splashy "splunk" in a glide below. The line mended to a curve, and the plump nymph bounced along the bottom, skidding past likely lies before the leader finally straightened. Eventually I got the hang of it by making achingly swift forward and back casts that straightened the line better. Skipping from boulder to boulder, I could feel a strange euphoria building in me as I sent more casts into the pewter flow before me. It was a kind of dual presence of self that you sometimes feel when you are mesmerized, like you're outside of yourself in some spiritual fashion looking at your own actions. I was absorbed by the clamor of the spring torrent cascading over the rocks, the motions of my body as I sent the fly line slicing through the humid air, and the earthy fragrances from the damp woods bordering this busy, bustling stream. My trance was broken when my footing slipped as I tried to skip on to a rounded boulder a shade farther than my longest lunge. With one sneaker wheezing, I made my way downstream to a large pool created by a beaver dam. The flow of the water slowed considerably here, the surface of the pool nearly placid, as the water marched toward its destination in this section rather than charging as it did upstream. I stood still along the bank, first searching for rises and when none were evident, I sought out the deepest part of the pool as being the likeliest place a trout would hide. To my surprise, at the very center of the pool where I was intently focused, a beaver surfaced and began swimming toward me, oblivious to my stone-still presence. He was about two yards away when he finally detected me, and when he did, he signaled a dire warning with the slap of his paddle-like tail on the pool's surface before quickly descending to the bottom toward the entrance of his lodge. The waves rippled in all directions, completely wetting several softball-sized rocks closest to the water's edge and splashing forcefully several inches up the sides of the larger boulders. Whatever trout may have been in that pool surely took their cue from the shock waves. It was pointless to bother with another cast. The fading light in the gray sky above ordered my retreat. No fish on this little venture, but no disappointment either. Some moments of ecstasy and one close encounter. Already inebriated with memories that make you want to drink from these places again, I turned my back on the pool and headed toward the cabin. I vowed to return, perhaps better equipped and more thoroughly prepared.

*   *   *   *   *   *   *

The West Branch of the Delaware has been the salvation of many fishing trips for my friend Bob and me when we've made jaunts to the Catskills. I'm not referring to the tailwater fishery below the Cannonsville Dam that all the fly-fishing magazines feature but to the area above the dam where fewer travel to find fish. Located on the northwestern border of the region, it is my favorite part of the Catskills, largely because its rural character has been pretty much left untouched by the upscale influences of "summer people" who own vacation homes near ski areas and the more popular trout towns. Here, one dairy farm abuts the next for miles on either side of the stream, with only a thin riparian border shielding the stream along most of its course up to the headwaters. The river twists and braids among the cornfields and cow pastures with just enough intermittently spaced oaks, maples, and syc-amores to shade the banks to offer protection to fish and some solitude for the different drum angler. This is an unhurried stream in an unhur-ried valley. It is really marginal trout water with some hatchery fish planted by the state each spring that are usually taken out by the locals by Memorial Day along with a small but persistent tribe of wild trout if you know where to sniff them out. Below the trout water, smallmouth bass compete with the coarse fish for a different kind of fly-fishing fare.

A couple of summers ago, on a late June afternoon, Bob and I ventured over to this section of the West Branch from our campground near Downsville. After fishing the East Branch hard for two days amid other anglers, campers, canoe traffic, and the like, we decided that we had to get away from everybody else who was getting away from it all. After packing our gear into his van, we plotted the route over to this less-regarded stream. The road over the mountain winds and twists past a sweeping view of bucolic pastures below, and an auto graveyard that seems decidedly out of place, yet at the same time strangely logical. This is "car-up-on-blocks" country, and the only places you leave old heaps are barns and broken-down pastures. We crossed the river and followed the road past an octagon-shaped farmhouse to a turn-off down an unpaved farm lane. A dowdy, barn-red, covered bridge spans the river here, providing a classic setting. After we parked in a nearby pull-off, I walked back to the bridge and went inside to peer out one of those conveniently placed openings that the prudent bridge builders always seemed to include in the architecture of these relics. Even 150 years ago, the best vantage of a stream was from the middle of a bridge, so a window-sized opening cut into the walls of the structure was a fitting finish to these otherwise utilitarian constructions. Upstream, a large pool formed behind dense boulders scattered across the river before the water passes under the bridge. As I surveyed the water, I noticed a few scattered rises pocking the stillness of the surface all the way to the head of the pool, 150 yards upstream. It had rained heavily the night before, and the river was receding from the higher water earlier in the day. The slight discoloration actually made conditions even better. The fish would be on the feed, and you could approach closer than in low-water conditions. We set up our rods and planned our strategy. A hike upstream to the second riffle ahead of the pool seemed in order while working our way back to the bridge. In the glide below that riffle, fish were boiling sporadically, taking emergers. No bugs escaped the surface yet, so we couldn't be sure of what was moving them. I let Bob take the lead, waiting until he was about thirty yards below me before I started fishing. I tied on a weighted #16 all-purpose brown and tan nymph, a fly that imitates almost any kind of mayfly nymph that might be involved in benthic drift after a high-water situation. A steady riser, coming up about every thirty seconds, caught my attention twenty-five feet from the bank. I dropped the nymph several feet in front of him and let it drift by. The fish did not move. I repeated the cast several more times with the same result. Thinking that I could get him to take the fly on the upswing, I moved above him a few yards. Still no look. After what seemed to be about thirty more casts, I gave up on what I assumed to be a very stubborn trout. I moved downstream and noticed that Bob had one on. He briefly played and then released what looked to be a twelve-inch brown. He looked my way and we both waved, but neither of us broke the silence. I cast my fly down and across, pulling off more line while mending it to allow the fly to sink to the bottom before I let the line tighten. At the end of the drift, as the fly was lifting off the bottom, a strong strike had me vainly trying to set the hook. Things were beginning to make sense though: We were in the early stages of a hatch, and most of the fish were taking nymphs just as they were leaving the bottom. The few that made it to the emerger stage were being picked off near the surface, explaining the sporadic rises and the absence of any winged adults on the surface. I let out another cast, feeling confident that the fly size was right, and the color did not matter. This time when the fly lifted from the bottom, there was a sharp tug. I struck quickly, hooking solidly into a fish. It turned and bulled to the center of the stream, twisting to one side of the current and then the other. After a minute or so of struggle, it surfaced and shook vigorously. As I played him closer, my elation quickly faded. On the other end of the line was a repulsive, sixteen-inch fallfish, which I like to erroneously refer to as "chubs." One that gave a good account of itself, but not a centerfold fish. I wondered if that was what Bob had caught earlier. Had he been holding out, too? Were we into a head of chubs instead of trout? Would they be fellow travelers, or were we just in chub heaven? Bob moved around a bend, and I stayed put, having had two hits in a row, even if one of them turned out to be the ugly stepsister rather than the lovely princess. I dropped another cast in the current, letting the fly bump along the bottom until it lifted at the end of the drift. Another strong take—third in a row—and I set the hook, this time nonchalantly playing the fish as I was prepared for disappointment one more time. The fight was more furious though, and two minutes of struggle ended with a beautiful wild twelve-inch brown resting in my palm. I quickly unhooked the fish and admired its regal stature. Whether out of surprise or out of the realization that no matter how many of these fine fish I have caught, I still found myself marveling at the fully formed fins, the yellow-bronze belly, and the rich, red-and-black discs dispersed across the back of a stream-bred brown. The fish quickly darted from my hand when I lowered him into the smooth current, fleeing to the safety of the deeper water. A few more fish were working at the bend where Bob had disappeared. I made my way down to that spot and could see by the slowing of the currents that the riverbed dropped off to a deep hole. I thought that Bob had moved through this section too quickly, and I intended to fish it more thoroughly. A few of the flies started breaking through the water now, Dark Cahills fluttering slowly to the overhanging tree branches, like miniature angels being summoned to the heavens. Feeling secure that the fish would continue to feed below the surface, I stayed with the nymph. The next cast placed the nymph above the drop-off. I felt it scraping the bottom as it drifted downstream. As it approached the hole, a vicious tug startled me and caused me to momentarily lose control of the rod. Line spun off the reel as the fish charged downstream. I regained an awkward grip on the rod as I put light pressure on the reel. Fearing that the 5x tippet would snap to the unyielding strength of this powerful fish, I let it take me to the backing. I kept the tension on the line, feeling the fish turning its head side to side, trying desperately to shake the cursed hook. After swerving across the current a few times, the fish began to tire. Playing him off the reel, I started to bring him gradually toward me. Turning to my left, I noticed Bob about seventy-five yards below and decided to breach our unspoken pact. "Yo Bob, I need the net," I yelled, motioning to the back of his vest where the only net between us was attached. Quickly realizing that I was serious, he began reeling in his line and started trudging upstream. He had a difficult time making his way back in the high water. Meanwhile, the fish gave grudgingly, advancing toward me after several stabs into the stronger currents. I suspected it was just about played-out after it lunged over to the slower water on my left. Bob was still fifty yards away, and I was apprehensive about keeping him on the line until Bob got up to me, so I decided to land the fish without the net. The muscular brown, a wild mature adult, came willingly now, and when he swam lazily near my knees, I reached into the silted water and grasped him. My hand barely cupped his bulging, wide belly and I hoisted him in the air for Bob to see. "A brown. Seventeen inches," I yelled proudly, "and maybe three pounds." As I let the words slip out, the fish, I suppose eager to get his pride back, thrust his body vigorously, breaking my grasp and plopping into the water. In doing so, he had broken the tippet and began sweeping powerful strokes with his tail, managing to clear the shallows and head toward the main current. I watched as the regal fish disappeared, feeling regret—not that he escaped, as I would have let him go anyway, but disappointed in the unglamorous release. Bob stopped, questioned me on why I didn't wait for the net after I summoned him, and without lengthy lecture forgave my lapsed judgment. After flurries of action with many hook-ups, we each touched around a dozen fish in the two hours that it took us to make our way back to the covered bridge. It was one of those occasions when all the elements of good fortune in fishing converge: ideal water conditions, a spectacular hatch, and perfect timing. And it came to an end quickly. Thunder echoed in the distance as storm clouds approached from the west. A breeze began to stir, bending the immature oats planted in the neighboring field in the same direction, causing the tops to droop over each other. By now, the dusky little angels were pouring out of the stream, and fish were swirling the surface in glorious feed. We wanted no more from this day so we broke down the rods, peeled off our waders, and made our way to the portal in the bridge for one last chance to bestow our gratitude on an overlooked Catskill stream. Wind-propelled raindrops splattered the windshield as we pulled out of the parking area. A quarter mile up the road, the downpour obscured all detail, and we crept out of the valley on the winding road to Downsville. At the summit of the final mountain before our descent to the East Branch, the sun momentarily broke through. I motioned to Bob that we should pull over for a moment. We both got out of his van and leaned against the side. Gazing toward the east, I pointed and whispered, "Look, there it is." He scanned in that direction, saw the sharply colored arc, then bumped my elbow. "Another one about thirty degrees above the first. A double rainbow." The higher one was less distinct, but clearly visible, and the sight of a pair of rainbows arching parallel to each other in the same sky was astounding. We stared, spellbound, for several minutes, not wanting to speak, as if afforded a profound revelation. Then, with little notice, sullen storm clouds quickly shouldered the surrounding mountains with a foreboding warning for the valley below.

*   *   *   *   *   *   *

It would seem heresy to devote a chapter to the Catskills without mentioning the Beaverkill and Willowemoc. I won't commit one here, but these are anything but less-traveled streams. In fact, their junction is considered the Mecca of Catskill destinations. As such, many pilgrims descend and rightfully so. Bob and I were among them one Memorial weekend when we camped at the state campground along the Beaverkill among the sinners from Babylon who were blasting raucous cassettes and chugging wicked beverages derived from fermented grains. It was our first fishing trip to the Catskills and, as neophytes, we invited this happenstance through our own ignorance. Luckily, most were not there to fish, so we were able to find some peace along the streams—too much peace, in fact. Heavy rains earlier in the week rose the rivers to nearly unfishable conditions. At the catch and release section of the Willowemoc, the river was full and bristling. Wading bordered on treachery. Only two others were brave (foolish?) enough to fish this stretch. A local who came down to the river for a look said he never bothered when the stream was this high. It yielded only one hit between us. We moved on to Cairn's pool, the only place where the water slowed enough to allow measured casts. Trouble was, everybody who had any fishing sense held the same idea. Cars were parked all along this section of Old Route 17 as if it were the staging area for some kind of spiritual cleansing. Well-attired disciples stood on the banks eagerly awaiting someone else to give up their stake in the crowded pool, like the hordes of bathers gathered on the banks of the Ganges. We got out of the van, kneeled, genuflected, and then drove on to higher ground.

*   *   *   *   *   *   *

September is the last act of the play that is trout season in the Catskills. Oh, you could go to one of the few sections of specially regulated water to continue your fishing if you really felt compelled, but I never travel up to the Catskills after the close of trout season at the end of September. For one thing, I like exploring the open water for discoveries of wild trout and searching for places where grad-school fish dodge the crafty exploits of seasoned bait-fishers. There's an added dimension to the challenge of fly-fishing when you fish up against the end of the season. The vacation assault has passed, and you can almost sense a sigh of relief from the mountains themselves as the region takes on a more serious tone. The mountains have nearly spent their allocation of precious water and smaller streams that ran dauntless in the spring are now meager trickles, confining skittish, fearful remnant trout to the low, clear pools. Larger rivers look exhausted, meandering slowly toward their pelagic destinies, as if slowing time with their passive currents. The close of the season forces you to be cognizant of the boundaries of your chances to legally fish for a beloved trout, making the opportunity more precious, the time more memorable. I seem to recall the last outing of each season with more clarity and greater passion and treasure it through the winter as a hoarded, old coin. There is always that last rise, that last cast, the last sweep of the fly in the current, and the hope that the fish who refused will be there next year. The rusts and yellows in the leaves at month's end will usher in the Catskill fall. The harvests and the frosts will take their turns at prominence before yielding to winter's cruel abeyance.

Many years ago, before I quit a job that was getting increasingly stale, I had to go to Albany in late September on some business travel. Or more accurately, I schemed that trip to Albany two months in advance because I knew I would have to travel through the Catskills to get there. My wife Carol wanted to come along for this one, and we would share a couple days together away from the ordinary responsibilities of work and home. These kinds of trips rejuvenate your relationship, especially when you surround yourself with the pleasant distractions of country roads, allowing you to reacquaint yourself with the person you were drawn to when first smitten, who somehow becomes too familiar when you're raising a family and fending off everyday trials. We took the back roads to my favorite area of the Catskills, leading us eventually to Delhi, the sleepy little town straddling Route 10 on the province's outer reaches. I wanted to come here to stir some memories and maybe create a few if the conditions were right. We chatted furiously, oblivious to the time, coasting through the northern tier of Pennsylvania by early afternoon. The trip was refreshing, and we looked forward to landing at the little motel overlooking the town. By the time we crossed into New York, the weather had taken a turn as cold gusts swept in from the northwest. When we were a few miles out of Delhi, another ominous sign befell us. What sounded like the exploding of a shot from a deer rifle was the right rear tire quickly deflating. It was probably the last flat

I remember changing in quite a while. With one of those thin, dough-nut-shaped spares that makes the car look as if it has polio, we hobbled into town, too late to get a repair at the only garage. We hunkered down for the evening in the stark, narrow motel room, constantly reminded of the chill outside by the monotonous drone of the fan motor on the wall-mounted heating unit. The cold wind constantly rattled the brittle pane of glass affording the only view out of our little compartment, reminding me how much sooner the foreboding winter comes to these Catskill valleys compared to the relatively mild reaches of downstate Pennsylvania. My wife and I snuggled in front of the cable TV, our only connection with the outside world, as if we were refugees from it.

My thinly veiled agenda for the next morning was a little excursion to the river—after the flat was fixed, of course. I had planned this migration months ago to close the New York trout season with one last day on a Catskill river. The weather was anything but willing. The wind calmed enough overnight to drop the temperature well below freezing, coating the valley in a heavy frost. As the sun rose, the crisp winds blew a succession of clouds over the mountains, looking as if it might snow or sleet. We took the car over to the garage. The owner assured us it would be done by eleven, giving us ample time to eat breakfast and wander about town. The wind continued fiercely, smothering my expectations, depressing my mood. One of the town roads led to a bridge over the river. We paused to look over the railing into a slow pool below. I could see intermittent dimples caused by feeding fish when the wind calmed long enough to allow the surface to settle. It gave me hope, but just as I thought about going out for the afternoon, several strong gusts kicked up, putting down the fledgling hatch, quelling the rises. It was the kind of wind that blows a fly line right in your face if you're casting into it and lifts your backcast into an ineffectual limp of line when it's behind you. I was despondent. I never considered, two months earlier on a sweltering July day, that I would be contending with a chilly, wind-whipped scourge to doom my fishing prospects.

After our walk, we still had time to kill, so we went back to the motel. My wife was content to read her novel. I stared out the window, first at the town below, then across the valley to the ridges to the north. On the bed, I gazed at the ceiling, then at the walls. I was being ravaged by the monotony, the utter disappointment. I dozed off to sleep momentarily, then awoke for no particular reason. The pace of the day was thrown off from the beginning. I needed to recover. I suggested a drive after the tire repair and Carol agreed. She could sense my desperation and knew it would be good for the both of us to get out of that contemptible little room.

Tooling around on the back-country roads in the Catskills has a strange attraction of its own. The power you have is the total control of where you want the car to go, without purpose or direction in mind. Rising out of a river valley in a steady climb toward higher terrain gives you the feeling of leaving the safe and secure for the unknown. At the first fork in the road, you decide left. At the next one, she decides right. Neither of you really care about the direction, but you both want to have a turn asserting yourself in give-and-take fashion, to see who can be the one to get the car to stumble across some interesting vista or local landmark. It's not a contest, though, as you know that all discoveries are accidental and you both take credit. Neither of you has been there before. It doesn't matter who drives, and you switch if the other insists. What's important is that you explore together, make decisions together, and weave the conversation based on what you encounter in front of you. She speculates on what it would be like to live on the isolated dairy farm you just passed, perhaps 140 acres of pasture and hay, with a dark-green carpet of clover surrounding the white clapboard home situated away from the road. The beauty and serenity are, you both agree, only skin-deep. You pass too many weather-scarred farms that reflect the dire conditions that portray the reality of carving out a living in the thin, rocky soil. It's hard to imagine what keeps people tied to these places, and then you look at the horizon through each window of the car and you know; these beautiful, bleak mountains are a pastoral purgatory that traps souls, a visual narcotic that requires a regular fix. You drive on, knowing that your life back home offers a comfort that you are not ready to trade, despite the wishful longing for the illusion of a less-burdened existence.

At midafternoon we pulled into Margaretville and lunched at a quaint little deli that we had to ourselves. The mood was both romantic and desolate at the same time—romantic because we felt special and catered to as if we were the only couple in love in the whole region and desolate for the same reason. We didn't feel like intruders or tourists so much as invisible voyeurs whose mission it was to observe the ordinary lives of locals, searching for little wisdoms as souvenirs to commemorate our modest excursion. We lingered until there were no more nuggets to gather.

We consulted a map for our next destination. It was up the road a piece and it would take us in a circuitous direction back to Delhi. We followed the East Branch of the Delaware as it parallels Route 30 north. The stream is a meandering meadow brook here, only about fifteen feet wide, crossing on either side of the highway until it finally disappears off to one side, away from the road near the town of Roxbury. A left turn up a steep grade on aptly named Hardscrabble Road brought us, in a short distance, past the boyhood homestead of John Burroughs. Farther up the road at the crest of the hill is his unmarked grave, denoted only by a memorial plaque as a state historical site. We got out of the car for a look. The brazen wind whipped furiously across the mountaintop as we made our way to the granite protrusion that he often used as an overlook. I was instantly attached to this man by way of that rock. I visualized the massive boulder jutting out into the Neshaminy Creek below the town of Hulmeville I often used as a perch when I was a young boy. For me, this was a place where introspection became important, and I gravitated to it often just to wistfully gaze on the stream as it curled by, stirred by my own natural surroundings. I imagined Burroughs, musing poised on his boulder, taking in the majestic view of the valley below. Carol was cold and headed back to the car. I continued to be intrigued and lingered, lost in my thoughts. Take away the paved roads and the vehicles and little has changed in the last hundred years from this vista. It is an eternal view, one that gives a permanent imprint of a bold, austere beauty. I sat on the rock, forging impressions about the unknown and unseen world beyond the ridges and peaks, as Burroughs must have when he felt summoned as a boy. The influence is strong here. The proud quiet strength exuded by the mountains, by this place, had me entranced. I stared at the sculptured mountains brushed by the hurried clouds, mesmerized by the expanse before me. I felt not just touched, but embraced, as if welcomed by a kindred spirit.

The wind reverberated against the silence as I got up from the rock and made my way back to the car, creating a whipping effect as if I were being ushered from this suspended animation back to real time. At the car I regained the present but had nothing to say. I felt detached from Carol until we started to drive. The humming of the tires on the gravel road descending into the valley slowly transformed my awareness, eventually bringing me fully in touch with her, with the car, and the Catskill mystique.

We arrived at the motel back in Delhi about five, my mood having shifted dramatically from the morning. So had the weather. The wind had calmed, and the bright horizon in the western sky glowed as the clouds disappeared. There were only about two hours of light left, but I felt a deep longing to get out on the water since we got here, so I decided to slip out during this last light for some final time on a Catskill stream, as we would be on our way to Albany the next day. I drove downstream to the familiar covered bridge and parked. The empty pull-off confirmed what I had suspected, that no one had ventured here lately. It was with Bob's unknowing blessing that I would come to our trusty little river. It looked different now, with fall stretching into the valley. Some leaves were already turning, a few had dropped, and the rest clung intently to their parent trees. Grasses along the roadside were tall, but thin. The brilliant greens of summer had faded. Goldenrod dominated the uncut fields, proudly displaying the rich, yellow flowers that warn of the end of trout pursuits. The blackberry bushes were thin and weary, and even the poison ivy leaves held a dry, reddish hue. The stillness was a stark contrast to the earlier day.

My rod slipped easily out of its case as I began to gear up. I fastened the reel before checking for worn leader. The last time I used it was a week before on a slow day on the Tulpehocken, where technical fishing of a size #22 tan caddis required a 7x tippet. After giving it the OK, I walked upstream, searching the water for any kind of disturbance, hoping I would find a hatch. About fifty yards upstream, I noticed some dimples on the far bank in some slow-moving water beyond the current. The water was low, though not too clear, enabling me to quietly wade to within casting distance. More fish started coming up, some closer to me in the smooth flow in the middle of the stream. A raft of blue-winged olive duns was drifting on the surface, wings upright as if a flotilla of tiny sailboats. Trout, some of them quite large, were sipping them effortlessly. A pod of about ten or so took up positions in feeding stations in the current next to the slack water, determined by their own sense of order. They were oblivious to me.

My trout flies are relegated to three fly boxes: the streamers, which usually don't see much action after April; the big flies, meaning anything size 16 and over, such as Cahills, Sulphurs, on up to hefty Slate Drakes; and the miniatures, those small caddis, BWOs, tricos, midges, and the like that I get the most use out of, particularly on the limestone streams that are among my home waters. Usually by this time of year, the tiny fly box looks like the last lonely boxes of a rummage sale, with flies scattered all over the place, defying the laws of order the larger flies willingly adhere to. I picked through the mess to find a #18 BWO floating nymph, that in-between fly that seems so succulent to surfacing fish. I tied it on to the tippet, pulled the fly a few times to make sure it was secure, and focused on the water. A sense of completeness was coming over me. I'm faced with a classic hatch of olives on a venerable, if less-loved Catskill river on the eve of a day where my emotions ranged from turbulent to sublime, from a monotonous little room to an expanse seemingly without time. It was a chance to put some finality to it all.

I stepped carefully into the water, eyeing the dimples, looking for the largest disturbance. I targeted a large trout, slurping in a constant rhythm, and false cast a few times behind it before letting the fly light upon the surface, about six inches in front of its nose. It floated lazily for a few seconds and then disappeared in another large ring. I struck firmly, though not too hard, aware that the light tippet could not be pressed. The fish headed downstream immediately, much to my good fortune, as he did not disturb any of the other feeders. I played him for a few minutes before bringing him to hand. His belly was yellowing near the pectoral fins, his spots a rich mixture of ruby and black. Recording the beauty of this wild, mature, fourteen-inch brown with a mental snapshot, I slipped the hook from his jaw and watched intently as he slowly disappeared in the glassy current. I took four more trout,

all in the twelve-to fourteen-inch range, each sporting the richly colored exteriors announcing their intent to spawn. The commotion of
their struggles caused the others in the pod to scatter. Upstream I
noticed another half-dozen fish positioned close to the bank. I considered stalking them, but there was no need. The river, this section of the
upper West Branch of the Delaware that I almost consider my private
water, had blessed me again, and I felt grateful. I scanned the surface
of the stream. The water slid along silently like a thin amber syrup, the
color and texture that slow-moving currents take on in the fall. Tracing
the far bank from my right slowly to my left, I absorbed the outline
of the rocky edges clogged with matted, wispy, dying grasses. The sun
crested on the western hills, smearing the blue sky with radiant gold.
The sycamores and maples on the stream's edge cast an enduring shade,
forecasting the evening's chill. I turned toward the bridge and began a
time-honored fisherman's retreat with the one thing I wanted to take
back with me: impressionistic sketches I could frame later.

8

Last Cast

Last cast. It is a phrase uttered to your fishing partner at the end of a fishing outing or one mentally issued to yourself when darkness has made it impossible to fish any longer, though the splashy rises of trout continue to lure you. At its best, it is the cast you are reluctant to make because, well, the fish are still rising, with hope being eternal. Sometimes it is the command you order to yourself when conditions broadcast to end fishing and end it now, perhaps due to an approaching storm or a relentless mosquito attack. Last casts happen at the end of an outing, the end of a journey to a far-off destination, the end of a season, and in all of our lives the concluding event that we know will arrive someday, often without any thought or planning. Regardless of the situation, last cast portends a serious, mindful moment not for its outcome but for its symbolic measure of our love and passion for fly-fishing. I find the most memorable last casts to be at the end of a season, when I've had a chance to mentally replay the fishing year in my head before reeling up one last time. It seems to be a clarion that becomes more pronounced the older and more experienced you are as an angler. I don't recall many memorable last casts as a youthful angler, but when you become more reflective about the fishing experience as a seasoned angler, the fishing passion yields to psychic markers as sacred introspective moments. There is something about finality that becomes important as you move through life.

When I was fishing the Tulpehocken Creek steadily in the early years of my fly-fishing development, the season for me generally started around the first of April when steady midge hatches brought up a decent number of trout and the year typically ended on the soft warm days of November, stretching to Thanksgiving most seasons. Usually you could count on tricos hatching right up until the first Arctic cold fronts would sweep in from Canada. I remember one particular season when the daytime temperatures approached the mid-60s right past the Thanksgiving holiday to the first day of December. The forecast for that day was ominous. Temperatures would approach 70 by midday, but an Arctic blast would drop them to near freezing by three in the afternoon. I saw it as my final outing, as a deep freeze would follow for more than a week. The air was still in the morning, and I decided to fish near the waterworks intake pipe. Few anglers ventured down there even though the pool held a fair number of sizeable brown trout. A small trico hatch appeared on schedule around ten in a cloudy, wind-free but exceptionally warm morning. In that section, I would fish upstream of the pool and let the fly drift first over any fish, not wanting them to see the 8X tippet attached to the fly. Fishing that way meant my back would be to the west, where the approaching weather would stage before forcefully arriving. I found myself looking behind every few minutes, as if trying to estimate when I should get off the water. Fish were rising sporadically, and I took a few nice browns while pinching a few others. About noon, I could see dark clouds seriously gathering for the predicted event. Wanting to stay until the last possible moment, I kept fishing. Within a half hour, the stillness broke, and a fierce gale whipped the surrounding trees while immediately chopping the water. The season was over. I had taken it right to the edge.

When my desire for wild trout became a more pronounced part of my fishing forays, I usually ended the season on the Little Lehigh Creek. It is a rather popular stream that has its headwaters on South Mountain near Mertztown and turns east where it picks up a cold spring to become a very good limestone fishery for most of its length. Most anglers know the section where it enters the park system of the city of Allentown as a one-mile fly-fishing-only designation, restricting the fishing by method and the absence of harvest. If you are willing to get off the beaten path, there are several stream segments that are under-fished that hold decent amounts of wild trout—mostly browns—though you can turn up a few wild rainbows, the progeny of stocked fish. My usual season-ending location was pretty much untouched by anglers most years, as signs with harsh wording prohibiting dumping and advertising heavy fines seem to discourage even parking. But there were no signs that stated, "No Trespassing" or "No Fishing," so I always took it as an invitation. With weather forecasts of recent years being fairly accurate with respect to temperature, wind conditions, and storm arrivals, I would usually try to ascertain my last fishing day when temperatures approached 60 degrees and calm winds, if those conditions preceded storms or a cold front that would usher in lasting discomfort. Ok, I'm a weather sissy—sue me.

One particular season ending I recall on that less-travelled portion of the Little Lehigh came about with the last pleasant day in November, right around the Thanksgiving holiday. I arrived at the pull-off a little after noon for a leisurely paced foray from the top of the section. A soft glide marks the beginning, and there are usually a few fish taking up positions at the end of the current before a long slow-moving pool. This is typically the blue-winged olive time of the year, and a couple of fish were working when I approached the water. Most of the leaves of the deciduous trees in the riparian buffer had been shed, so ample light cast across the stream, causing a slight glare as I looked downstream. Those fish at the head of the pool were quite willing, and I took a few on a blue-winged olive floating nymph. It seemed as if my early success would forecast a respectable day on the stream, but not so. For the next few hours I inched downstream, casting to the occasional rise. Though conditions were perfect, few fish were working, and the ones that positioned themselves behind fallen trees or logs made casts or drifts nearly impossible. My plan was to slowly fish all the way downstream to the next posted property then work my way back up, hoping to encounter new risers in the reverse direction as well. It's a methodical approach that I usually find successful when blue-winged olives hatch sporadically. In any case, I proceeded slowly to the end of the segment before making my way back upstream without having caught another fish. As the sun started to lean against a small, tree-covered hill to the west, the light was fading, signaling the end of this venture. About midway back I decided to change tactics, really more out of frustration then applying any scientific method to the conditions. I cut back to 4X tippet and tied a large, weighted, soft hackle wet fly, a #10 nondescript charcoal number that I typically use in early spring as a searching pattern for more gullible, hungry trout waking out of winter doldrums. When I stepped out on a rock cropping, I could gauge a deep pool to my left with a subtle current leading to it, about thirty feet away. Seemed like the best place to drop a fly, and I did. A few seconds after the fly sunk, the current took it to the end of its swing, and a sudden strong tug telegraphed a sizable fish. Out of the quiet pool, a sixteen-inch rainbow blasted like a rocket two feet above the surface before crashing back down. After another reckless jump, the fish finally relented and began his reluctant ride toward my outstretched hand. I held the fish up to the fading light, admiring the crimson streak across his lateral line before letting it go. It was one of those rare last casts that ended the season with a considerable fish.

My final couple of last casts in Pennsylvania were made on the Manatawny Creek, a tributary to the Schuylkill River in eastern Berks County. Our place before we moved to Oregon was situated in the Manatawny watershed. In fact, a small tributary to the Manatawny flowed along the edge of our property. It was too small to fish, but it did hold wild brown trout that you could sometimes spot in deeper pools when conditions were right. In the last two years before we moved, I knew we would be selling the house, so I decided to stay in the watershed for the last trips to a trout stream for the season's end. The Manatawny holds both wild and stocked trout, with thermal impairments in the upper reaches caused by poor agricultural practices, the limiting factor in reproduction. Nonetheless, trout can be located in most sections of the stream once the cooler weather of fall arrives. In October of 2012, a little after mid-month, I went out for a pleasant afternoon of fishing, not thinking anything about last cast, as the cooperative weather typically stretched well into November. What I remember most about the outing was the location I chose. It was near a bald eagle nest that was established two years earlier. To get to one of the better stretches on the stream, you had to creep past a large sycamore that contained the nest at the top of the tree. No matter how discreet you tried to maneuver, if the eagle was in that tree, it was going to announce a warning with a high-pitched, whittling screech. That never affected the fishing, but nearby fledglings might get the message that danger was afoot. That particular day turned up a few wild browns in the ten-inch range. Nothing special, but a pleasant day. What became memorable was the rapid descent into winter. The early part of the next week turned blustery and cold—not necessarily unusual, as that kind of weather is often followed by warm, windless days. Not so that year. On Halloween, a twelve-inch snow-fall surprised everyone and knocked out power for long periods in that rural location when the heavy, wet snow brought down many trees. The rest of November issued wet, cold weather. My leisurely day in October produced the earliest last cast of my fly-fishing experience. Sometimes you just never know when that last one is coming.

*　　　*　　　*　　　*　　　*　　　*　　　*

Opening Day of trout season in Pennsylvania has been a tradi-tionally celebrated event for those who primarily seek stocked trout planted a few weeks before the season starts. I had not participated in one since I was a teenager when my parents drove me to the Neshaminy Creek above Langhorne. Once I embraced fly-fishing, I never bothered. Many of the special regulations waters had year-round fishing with har-vest restrictions, so there was no need to pay attention to the opener. Besides, I wasn't about to go jousting among the table fare crowd to fit in a little combat angling. Fly-fishing among the hoopla of campers surrounding smoldering fires, gathering worm containers and scented fish eggs, or attaching red and white spoons to twelve-pound test line would be akin to attending a poetry reading amongst a throng of pro-fessional wrestlers.

Then one year something stirred me to go out on Opening Day to unprotected water after my long, self-imposed absence. I'm not sure if it was a nostalgic reach back to childhood, or whether there was some sense of masochistic ritual to be celebrated, but I felt that being on unreg-ulated water was an observance I should be part of. Not that this partic-ular Opening Day was the first time I would be out that season, because it wasn't. On a warm mid-March Sunday about three weeks earlier, I was among hundreds of fly-fishing brethren on the catch-and-release section of the Little Lehigh where a hatch of stoneflies and midges celebrated an advanced edition of spring.

Having accepted the notion that I would find myself on open water that third Saturday in April, I prepared myself by sleeping in until 9:30, long after the starting bell. There was no sense of urgency. Vegetable beds needed turning prior to the spring planting, so I tended to that and a few other garden chores before rounding up my gear. The day was overcast and cool, the dampness of the previous night's rain clinging to the raw air. I threw my gear in my van and took off, heading north. My first thought was to go to a pretty little stream that is not stocked but may have a few wild browns that wander down from a Class A section several miles upstream. I nixed that idea though, because the weather was not going to cooperate with the bugs. That stream doesn't have great hatches, and I needed to have a stream I could count on. If there's anything I hate, it's dredging a parade of nymphs through hatchless water. The Little Lehigh is a limestoner with decent olive and caddis hatches at that time of year but can get a little crowded in the early season. I headed toward it. As I was driving, I was mentally preparing myself for minor skirmishes there when I decided to take a detour. I remembered a small creek at the headwaters of the Perkiomen where I noticed a rise in a pool near the road when I was on one of my scouting missions two weeks earlier. And I had heard some rumors about wild trout in there. Deciding that it would be better to fish a questionable stream in relative peace than fend off restive fly anglers, I turned off the main road and followed a farm lane until it met the Hosensack Creek, that headwaters tributary I had never fished. Just beyond a small iron bridge, I turned my van off the road into a muddy, well-worn parking area and came to a rest immediately in the soft, moist ground. I sat there a minute with the motor turned off and realized that there was something very different within me this day. At that stage in my fishing ritual, I was usually very obsessed with getting as much time on a trout stream as possible, fishing it incessantly, and counting fish caught as if the numbers represented a fishing competency that had to be achieved for it to be a good day. Instead, in the late morning I meandered to a stream of relatively minor consequence in the great trouting scheme of things. My pace slowed to reflect the prominence of the stream, or more likely the value of downshifting. I drew in a lengthy breath, then exhaled in a barely audible drone. The feeling was release and relief, one of those experiences in your life that you can look back on and acknowledge as having greater significance than the actual event. I was ready to enjoy the process of fishing instead of the outcome. It was a different kind of being alive. I looked around. The parking lot was empty, so obviously no stocked fish or their worshipers were present here. *I'm all alone,* I thought. *I've got Opening Day solitude, almost a contradiction in terms, and maybe some small trout in a headwater stream. I'll go to where I saw the rise earlier.* Just as I got out of the van, I noticed an elderly farmer in bib overalls, a tan porkpie hat cocked sideways across his brow, strolling from his nearby house to the stream. As he approached the stream, he stared over the bridge, leaning a stubby spin cast rod on the guardrail, eyeing the very location where I spotted the rise a few weeks earlier. He knew about that trout. Of course he did. They were neighbors and I was an outsider visiting their secluded refuge. I stood and watched from a distance while sifting the back of the van for my rod case. The farmer never acknowledged me, though I knew he was aware of my presence. He bent over and reached into his bait container and began tossing what appeared to be small mealy worms into the water, one every few seconds apart. The old gent was chumming that neighbor trout! Creating a mealy worm hatch, softening him up for the one spiked mealy worm that the trout would regret for the rest of his short life. I smiled and felt a kind of odd affinity for the old farmer. We were polar opposites on the fishing spectrum, but we were united by a common purpose on that cool, gray afternoon. We both wanted to catch a trout or two in peaceful, uncomplicated circumstances on this narrow, neglected little stream.

I watched for several more minutes and then took out my rod case. The two rods I brought along were a 7'6" two-weight for small streams and an 8'6" four-weight for larger water. The two-weight would be perfect here. I fastened the reel and threaded the line through the guides. Only a couple of flies would be needed—some small, blue-winged olives, a few caddis, and a couple of tan and green nymphs would likely serve me well. I deposited them into a small fly box and stuffed it into my vest. Downstream might produce a few larger pools, I thought, so I headed that way. As I moved steadily with the flow of the current on the marshy berm, thickets of silky dogwood, witch hazel, and willows crowded the stream bank so densely you'd need brush hog to cast a fly there. Without waving the rod even once, I resigned myself to circling around on a nearby service road and headed upstream above the farmer.

That portion of the stream curled past a few clearings next to an abandoned pasture, and I knelt down by one of the pools searching for rises. There weren't any, and instead of putting on a nymph, I decided to head back downstream. There may have been a trout or two in that pool, but I had a change of heart. This day would be more for exploring and sizing up this stream rather than trying to fish it; that would have to wait for another time. As I headed back to the van, I came upon the farmer. He was perched quietly on the bank next to the bridge, but he had stopped chumming. By this time, I had realized what I liked about his style; patience was the essence of his tactics. Good fishermen learn patience early, since it is a virtue that gives you endurance when the

fishing is slow, which it mostly is on days like this one. When I sauntered up to him, we exchanged the usual pleasantries.

"Catch anything?"

"Nope."

"Me neither. Too bushy to use one of these," I offered, motioning
to my fly rod. I tried to ply him for more information about this place.
He gave in grudgingly.

"Ever take anything out of here?"

"Once in a while, I'll get one for me and the wife."

"I usually put 'em back," I said, not trying to look too high-minded.

"I put 'em back if they're small ones. Got to be twelve inches
for me."

I tried to look nonchalant while I reset my glance toward the
slow-moving water passing under the bridge. I couldn't believe this guy
was telling me he takes twelve-inch trout out of this little stream.

"The secret," he volunteered, "is to bring along clippers and trim
the bushes near the pools you want to fish. Then drop your line carefully
into the pool."

I knew I was never going to get involved in that kind of fishing,
but I had to respect his ingenious stalking methods. That's when I realized that I, as a modern fly-fisherman, was bumping up against a man
who represented the last remnants of rural culture in the area. It was
perfectly ordinary to walk from your house down to the stream, take a
couple of trout, and have the wife ready the pan for a rare luxury that
his tough existence offered. But this commonplace country experience
was soon to be but a memory for him.

"That your place over there?" I inquired.

"Yep," he answered, "but it won't be for long. I've got it up for sale."

"Oh, I didn't notice the sign."

"Don't have one. My son is taking care of it."

"How long have you lived here?"

"All my life," he replied as he stood there with a hint of pride piercing his stoic countenance. "I was born in the back bedroom on the second floor."

"How many acres?" I asked, looking up toward what was, on second glance, an unadorned old farmhouse with white wood siding surrounded by a small parcel of lush acreage.

"Sixty."

"Do you still farm it?"

"Not anymore. I rent it to a fellow over the hill."

"Where are you moving to?" I questioned, hoping for but not expecting to hear the answer I wanted.

"An apartment, probably in Allentown, where there's a bus line," he confessed. "I can't drive anymore, and the wife only has one good eye left. We don't have that much money."

As he spoke, I became pained by his words and inwardly saddened. Here was a man who spent his entire life toughing out an existence in what has become the last undeveloped land in these parts, having to throw in his cards when life dealt out a few too many bad hands. I tried to imagine his lifelong rural existence captured by that moment we shared— walks down a rugged country lane to visit neighborly trout; meditative moments by a familiar stream; the ache of distant barking dogs; stiff breezes that ruffle the leaves on the scruffy oaks; and the fragrance of fresh-cut clover. The shimmering reflections in the trout pool would gradually blur. In time they would be but a distant memory. I felt frozen knowing a part of that weary farmer was going to die the mournful day he sold that property. Feeling a loss for words and awkward at this point like you do at a funeral, I hesitated, searching vainly for the right thing to say. I wanted to leave this proud soul with the peaceful surroundings he came to enjoy alone for one of his last moments at this place.

"I'm sure you have many good memories of this place," I blurted falteringly as I tried to desperately to put a favorable slant on our exchange.

"It'll be hard to leave," he offered, assuming a graceful poise to offset my discomfort. We looked at each other with knowing glances. His anguish would someday be my own, as it will be for all passionate anglers who confront the painful moment when we have to lean a treasured rod against a wall for the last time. It almost makes you want to die in your waders, like the proverbial gunslingers. I quickly sobered, trying to deny that I felt any kind of bond with him.

"Well, I gotta go on to a bigger stream so I can swing one of these sticks a bit," I said as I shook my rod. "You have a good day."

"Thanks," he nodded.

Walking over to my van and placing the rod inside without taking it apart, I felt conscious of all my muscles collaborating to accomplish this simple task. My eyes scanned the parking area to drink in every detail of this damp woodland terrain. I inhaled the moist, thick air, then started the engine. The van rocked lazily over each rut in the path worn by previous treads, eventually turning on the road while I gave him one more nod and wave while crossing the bridge. As the van crawled slowly past the sturdy, rugged farmhouse, I reflected on our brief encounter. He never caught that trout, and I never even cast a fly. The fishing gods have sent me off to another stream and perhaps better fortune. I reckon they wanted to keep him there for his last cast.

9

Redeeming Currents

Therapist: So, you had a 'poor' childhood. What do you mean by that?

Patient: I had one pair of sneakers that had to last the whole year. By July, they had holes in the toes and rips in the insoles. I couldn't get another pair until school started in the fall.

Therapist: (shaking his head back and forth empathetically) That's terrible.

Patient: I had two brothers and two sisters. We each got one gift for Christmas.

Therapist: Oh my.

Patient: Not only that, we had only one car, a ten-year-old Ford station wagon. We never went on vacation, just day trips to the shore.

Therapist: (pausing to reflect) I'll bet you still had good times.

Patient: You're right. Not having money didn't mean anything as a kid.

Therapist: (nods approvingly) I see.

Patient: So what should I do?

Therapist: About what?

Patient: About money!

Therapist: It really worries you, doesn't it?

Patient: I'm terrified. I feel like I don't have any choices.

Therapist: (pauses thoughtfully) A wise man once told me, 'Embrace your bliss, and the money will follow.'

Patient: (appearing confused) Oh.

*　　　*　　　*　　　*　　　*　　　*　　　*

There are several Bushkill Creeks in Pennsylvania. The one I find most intriguing is a limestone-fed creek in the eastern part of the state with its terminus at the Delaware River in the city of Easton. It's known by locals as the "Little Bushkill," though I think it is nearly as big as the others. Easton is a small industrial town, or should I say a post-industrial town, these days. Its most notable company is Binney and Smith, the firm that makes Crayola Crayons. I think I can say without much exaggeration that practically every adult in America probably clutched a Crayola Crayon as a kid, and unless you had a bad experience with a kindergarten art teacher, the memories have been mostly kind. Their production facility borders the Bushkill on the outskirts of town along the catch-and-release section of the stream. They've established a partnership with the Forks of the Delaware Chapter of Trout Unlimited and have become good corporate neighbors. Easton's other claim to modern-day fame is as the home of Larry Holmes, a former heavy-weight boxing champion known in those circles as the Easton Assassin.

The Bushkill begins as a freestone stream off the south slope of Blue Mountain and does not pick up its limestone influence for another twenty miles, near the village of Stockertown. By looks alone, you would not be able to discern any difference in the stream at that point, as there is no evidence of the typical limestone characteristics: slow glides, fanning elodea, or watercress bunches along farm meadows. It continues to appear freestone in every other respect. Of late, major sinkholes have been developing in the creek bed draining the surface water. Some blame a quarry situated not far from the banks. Others note that there has always been an unstable geology due to limestone strata in that valley. I have not fished it in over a dozen years, but I have been told the problem has gotten much worse.

Where the surface water has stabilized is where the Bushkill reveals its true character, with the presence of wild, brown trout, thousands of them, and the insects upon which they feed. It is one of the most fertile streams in the whole state. The catch-and-release section is fished most often by knowledgeable locals. The fish are tough, and very wary. A local guide told me that fly anglers from New Jersey pass right by it and head to the stocked sections of the Little Lehigh where the fishing is easier. In a way, I can't say I blame them. The first few times I fished it, the trout got the best of me. By all rights I should have driven by it myself, but I'm one of those stubborn anglers who refuses to let a stream defeat him. I keep going back until I stumble across a few over-confident risers.

The pastoral character of the stream disappears under the Thirteenth Street Bridge, where it enters the core of the city of Easton. There, it's a refuge for the jaded angler, where overturned shopping carts line the banks, serving as impromptu stream-improvement devices for a derelict trout stream. Stocked trout are planted here and quickly rounded up by the early spring urban fisher folk, leaving their wild cousins to the few who venture into this unlikely haven. To me, "urban trout fishing" is almost a contradiction in terms, though it has a mystique to it that almost defies explanation. These are fish that thrive in the kind of places most fly anglers try to escape when they go on trout missions. Its curious water is bordered by old factories, junk yards, and abandoned lots, kind of like a rundown neighborhood that you go back and visit to remind yourself just how tough times were.

Trout water that flows through small, industrial cities seems to breed a distinct kind of angler, and the fly-fishers of these places are decidedly blue-collar, and usually some of the best you'll ever come across. That's probably because their modest budget usually only affords them time on a heavily fished river with incredibly experienced trout— furtive, suspicious, downright brilliant specimens. Fish that can tell you where you bought your hooks, how much the feathers cost, and how long it took to tie the fly. I consider them a training ground for the technical elite. The Little Bushkill is that kind of water.

The last time I seriously fished that creek was 2008. I was in the catch-and-release section, looking down from a bridge into the stream, as anglers are often wont to do before fishing a piece of water. It was late July, and the morning Trico hatch was nearly over. I gazed upon a serious eighteen-inch wild brown intermittently nosing the film. He positioned himself in front of a submerged boulder about the size and shape of a living room recliner. I had fished that stretch several times earlier that year and often cast my fly over rises in that vicinity, but never took the time to look over the bridge to gain insight into the water, the resident brown, or the surrounding eddies and currents. As it turns out, the water currents were complicated. A tippet had to have considerable slack for the fly to ride out the swirls in the braided flow for a drag-free drift. The problem, of course, was that the extra slack was inevitably visible to the fish. From this perfect lie, a fish could detect an artificial every time. You couldn't even get a refusal from that fish. Everyone I'd talked to confronted the same situation. No one had ever known this fish to be taken. One of those proletariat fly-fishers I referred to earlier, an old guy who fished the stream for forty-six years, just shook his head in begrudging respect when I pointed out that deceitfully clever specimen.

Later that same year, in early October, I found myself going back to the old neighborhood—directly under the Thirteenth Street Bridge to be exact. A morning caddis hatch had the fish stirring and several were rising in a small pool beneath the bridge in a side channel. I took a few eleven-inchers right away. Larger fish gave me refusals at first, and then never bothered. Still, I concentrated on taking one, casting repeatedly over the rise forms of a sizable brown picking off tan duns in a steady rhythm. In the middle of a backcast, my concentration was broken by the decided sloshing of water behind me. I turned around, annoyed at what I expected to be an inconsiderate angler passing me for better water upstream. My annoyance became dismay when I saw a young Afro-American kid, about eleven years old, stomping toward the middle of the stream, wetting his jeans to mid-thigh. I ignored him at first, hoping he would go away.

"How ya doin' mister?" he quizzed as he made his way next to me. "Catch anything?"

"Got a couple," I muttered lowly.

"Can I see 'em?"

"No, I put them back."

As the water settled, I prepared to cast again. The browns stopped rising, and the prospects seemed dimmer.

"I want to see you catch one."

"So do I. You have to be quiet and still to catch fish," I sternly suggested, hoping that he would take the hint and leave.

"I brought my rod, but nothing was biting. It's over by my bicycle." He pointed to a battered bike laying in the soft mud of the bank. A spinning rod of equal caliber was laying across it. It intrigued me to see this kid interested in fishing. My perception of recreation for young, Black kids from impoverished backgrounds was of playgrounds and school yards with basketball courts and busted glass, where innocence is quickly swallowed by the gangs and drugs of their older counterparts. The kid obviously lived close by, and I surmised that streams like this one, which had an attraction for me when I was that age, have a stronger pull than I imagined.

"When are you gonna get one mister?"

"I'm not. Not here anyway. They're done biting." I reeled in my line and headed for the bank. The kid was becoming a pest, I decided. *I work hard*, I rationalized, and I deserved some undisturbed time on the stream. My decision to drive the three-quarters-of-a-mile up to the catch-and-release section was an easy one. I stepped on to the bank and walked past the bicycle. He stomped out of the water and leaned over to pick up the bike.

"Where are you going now?"

"Up the stream a bit," I countered, trying not to reveal too much.

"You know, I have a rod like that." He motioned to mine as he lifted the bike out of the mud.

"A fly rod?"

"Yeah. My parents got it for me for my birthday."

I had a hard time believing the kid at this point. He didn't seem like the type to know about fly rods, and I really doubted he knew what he was talking about. I patronized him anyway.

"You ought to bring it down to the stream some time."

"I will," he responded.

"Look, I'm going to drive farther upstream. I'll see you later."

"Okay, mister."

I drove upstream to the next bridge, the one where the big, scholarly brown resides. Standing next to the bridge pillar, near the glide that feeds his refuge, I scanned the water, hoping for a glimpse of his leathery snout breaking the surface. He was not moving at this point, but several splashy rises in the lower section revealed his neighbors to be on to the hatch. I shuffled down to the stream and began fishing the #20 tan caddis dry that I had on earlier. In three casts, I took two fish, again about eleven inches each. I saw several other rises on the far bank and prepared to cast to the one closest to me.

"Hi, mister!"

I looked to my left up at the bridge. I knew who it was immediately.

"I brought my fly rod. Want to see it?"

He didn't wait for my answer. He skipped over the guard rail, hoisting the rod behind him, and made his way to the edge of the stream near the end of the glide.

"I'm not sure how to use it. I tried it a couple of times, but I never caught anything with it."

"They're hard to use." After being such an ass, I relented. "Here, let me see it."

We exchanged rods, and I held his heavy, Fiberglass, discount-department store rod in my hand briefly. The whole set—rod, reel, and inexpensive level taper line—probably set the kid's parents back twenty-four bucks. I inspected the leader and tippet. It was one piece of monofilament about twelve-pound test, far too heavy and stiff for the kind of fishing offered in the Little Bushkill. On the end of the leader was what looked to be a #14 dark-brown caddis emerger, the only passable item in the whole outfit. I tried casting the rig. A clothesline prop had more action than this rod. I felt sorry for the kid. He was obviously looking for a mentor. We traded rods again.

"You'll probably catch something with this. Stand over there. See that water, running smoothly past that boulder in the water? It's called a glide. It's a good place to fish. Cast your line out toward the middle. See what happens."

"Thank you, mister. Think I'll catch anything?"

"You've got a good fly on here. It's called a 'caddis.' You never know with fishing. Some days you have good luck, some days you don't."

He calls me mister. Nice kid. I watched as he prepared to cast. He was a little sloppy, but his first few casts were quite passable. His line was getting out to the middle.

"Nice cast," I reassured. "Let the fly drift all the way over to there. Then pick it up and cast again, upstream, toward that fast water. That's called a riffle. The fish wait for food where the riffle meets the glide. Be really quiet. Don't wade unless you have to. Fish don't like to be disturbed."

With that encouragement, I prepared to cast again. We were a stark contrast in styles, literally worlds apart. I cast an expensive Orvis rod, wore a well-equipped vest, and shielded my pale, hairy thighs with trim-fitting waders. The kid, casting a department store standard issue, stood in the chilly water in his sneakers and jeans. But he was doing okay, casting the rig sufficiently to get the feel of what it is like to fly-fish.

And he was being still enough to allow the rises on the far bank to reappear. I felt self-congratulatory, like I did my part for humanity or something. I concentrated on the rises, occasionally peaking over at the kid. He obviously wasn't going to catch anything, but at least I was giving him some pointers, some stuff that he could use later if he somehow continued to pursue the sport.

I put a cast near a rising fish. To my left, I heard a large fish break the water, followed by an excitable yell.

"I got one, mister. He's big!"

My God, the kid's got one on. Must be a chub. They get big sometimes, but they're awfully stupid.

"Just keep the line tight," I yelled. "Pull it in with your left hand as the fish comes to you."

The bend in the Fiberglass pole told me the kid had a sizable fish on. It went upstream and jumped again. About eighteen inches. The monarch of the pool. The fish that nobody could take. The kid had the damned thing on the end of his twelve-pound tippet. It started to move swiftly downstream, toward me. I brought in my line to prevent a tangle. The kid was doing a good job of playing the fish. It jumped again and headed toward him.

"Pull in your slack. Keep the line tight."

The kid did as I instructed. As long as he kept a tight line, I figured he wasn't going to lose the fish. The leader was too big, too strong to allow that. After another minute or two of play, the fish tired near his knees. He reached down with both hands, cradling the rod under one arm, and hoisted the bruiser out of the water. His arms wrapped around the fish like a toddler clutching a teddy bear. A smile streaked across his face after he realized what he had accomplished. Fact is, he really didn't realize what he had accomplished. No one I talked to could entice that fish in those tricky currents. He outperformed all the proficient anglers I came across on that little river. I reluctantly offered the next piece of advice.

"You can't keep fish here. You have to put them back." He looked at me incredulously, still hugging the fish.

"But how will anyone know I caught him?"

"I'm your witness. I saw it." I felt a sense of shame for insisting the kid return the fish. It was a trophy of sorts. And I'm sure the kid would have a hard time convincing his peers or his family of what he had done. A part of me could visualize the kid riding off with the fish dangling from his handlebars, turning heads as he rode home. He'd cause great commotion riding down his block past the half-court basketball games, the tired mothers sitting on stoops, and men repairing downtrodden cars. I was taking all that away from him, denying his moment of triumph. The kid reluctantly dislodged the hook and stooped low to the water, gently releasing the fish.

"Nobody's gonna believe me."

"I know you caught that fish. It's the biggest one caught here this year. You should be proud." I tried to offer encouragement, but it felt hollow even to me. Both of us fished for another fifteen minutes. The rises had all stopped, the water was dead. The sun glared sharply on the water.

"I think the fish have stopped biting. The hatch is over."

We climbed up the bank over the guard rail and crossed the bridge, heading for the parking area. I couldn't bring myself to look over the edge.

"I guess I'll see you around here again," I reluctantly offered.

"Where do you live, mister?"

"About an hour from here. Around fifty miles."

"That's far."

"Yeah. Hey, what's your name anyway."

"Roy."

"Okay, Roy. I'll see you around. And hey, you outfished me today. Good going."

The kid lowered his head and offered a modest smile as he sauntered toward his bike while I started to break down my gear at the van. Suddenly I felt compelled to give him something, as a kind of gesture acknowledging our shared experience and his accomplishment. From my passenger seat, I opened my fly box and pulled out a neatly tied nymph and returned to the back of the van. Just that quickly, he disappeared. I ran to the road. I could see for almost a half-mile, down to the Thirteenth Street Bridge. There was no sign of him. I raced back to the van, quickly started the engine, and proceeded toward the bridge in hopes of catching a glimpse of him, but he was gone. He obviously melted into the surrounding neighborhood somewhere near the bridge. A sense of melancholy enveloped me. Dejected, I drove on, deciding to head home. On the highway, the incessant drone of the van's engine spurred me to sift through my feelings. There was no need for anguish, I resolved. He didn't need my fly, my hollow little memento. A remarkable little river probably expanded the aspirations of a marginalized Black kid uncovering one of its elusive treasures. In a just world, I suppose a fine trout is a kind of spiritual blessing for having holes in the bottom of your shoes.

10

Woodward Cave

(Piscator, Venator, and Siddhartha are seated on the ground under an expansive beech on a berm above a slow-moving, English chalk stream.)

Venator: So, what is the meaning of life?

Siddhartha (rhetorically): What if life has no meaning?

Venator: So, why are we here?

Siddhartha: To attain eternal light.

Venator: If life has no meaning, how can there be eternal light?

Siddhartha: Eternal light is a state of being.

Piscator: Perhaps eternal light is down by the river.

Venator (perturbed): You're trivializing our discussion.

Siddhartha: Not necessarily. Eternal light comes to you wherever you may be.

Venator (appearing confused): Yes, but spending all your time by the river like he does hardly describes attainment.

Siddhartha: That doesn't mean he won't experience it there.

Piscator: Truthfully, I never even think about it.

Siddhartha (exuding a peaceful smile): Then that might be the best place to let it come to you.

Venator: I think I missed something.

Siddhartha: It's simple. You can't search for eternal light. It comes to you. The river is as good a place as any.

*   *   *   *   *   *   *

For me, what defines a less-traveled stream is the mystery or discovery that the fly-fishing experience provides. If you go during the off season, when the hatches are as sparse as the crowds, even a famous stream like the Penns Creek becomes an off-the-beaten-track experience. I've found this to be the case on the upper Delaware as well, when I had the place to myself in the middle of the week in late September a few years back. Same goes for the Brodhead, a popular Pocono stream with an iconic fly-fishing past. But it isn't just the lack of crowds that makes the experience unique, but the mindset you bring to it. If you're consumptive about your fishing experience, then only catching fish—preferably big fish—matters. But if you go somewhere assuming you will be on a journey, your perspective shifts to wonder and adventure with some introspection thrown in for good measure. In the same way that we quantify and compare our fishing on a particular distant stream to others more familiar or close to home, our psychological packaging comes with us, whether we care to admit it or not, even when our desire is to "get away from it all." The feeling that overcomes us often when we are not catching fish is frustration because our expectations are the backdrop shading the fishing experience. And it is hard to go on a fishing journey to well-known rivers without some level of anticipation since these places have acquired a reputation for good reason, right? Changing and opening mindset, then, become a necessary prerequisite to advance the view that the fly-fishing journey will be adorned with unexpected pleasures or obscure rewards.

Every other year or so, I manage to fish the streams in the Penns Valley—the Pine, the Elk, and the Penns Creek—during the slow times of the year. The Pine and the Elk are small limestoners that make up the headwaters of the Penns Creek and are apt to have hatches of small caddis or blue-winged olives most mornings or evenings. The Penns also offers divine solitude when the green drakers have all packed it in for the season to head out to Montana. Outside of a few locals who fish in the evenings after work, I seldom come across anyone else trekking to this water in the hot breath of summer or the dwindling hatches of mid-September. There aren't many places to stay in that area (unless you own a cabin), so I usually find myself roughing it at the Woodward Cave Campground, an aged private facility that also serves as the only entrance to the Woodward Cave (fee for service, mind you). For me, roughing it generally consists of throwing a foam mattress on the floor of my cargo van with a sleeping bag for decor and added warmth. It affords the kind of aesthetics one aspires to on ten dollars a night, if you can put up with being relegated to the far end of a five-acre field, away from the more comfort-oriented crowd in tattered, aged RVs. There are a few rustic cabins closer to the cave entrance, but unless the weather falls apart on you, you'd consider it spoiling yourself if you went to that extreme. Oh, I'm not against spoiling myself, don't get me wrong, but if I have to decide between a comfy bed or a necessary piece of fishing equipment (I know—a redundancy), the cabin goes to the bottom of the list.

A few years ago, in late September on one of my Penns Creek sojourns, I pulled into the campground and went to register at the office. The property had apparently changed hands, and the guy at the other end of the counter had this sneaky grin and a strange twinkle in his eyes, like he just got away with defrauding a millionaire. He was about forty, medium height and build, with brown hair that curled on the top. We bantered a bit about the Penns Valley before I found out his name was Pete, and he had just sold another business to devote more time to the campground, apparently the result of the poor health of a relative who was the previous owner. The guy's affect was really strange, with a twinge of humor and a trace of sarcasm in everything he said. I wasn't sure if I was dealing with an agent of the devil or what, but I asked for the usual campsite on the far edge of the field and he happily obliged.

"By the way," I inquired, "what did you do before this?"

"Look at the truck on the way out," he replied with his characteristic gleam. The lettering on the side of the pickup reassured. "Pete's Satellite Systems" was scribed under the emblem of a TV satellite beamed toward the sky. This was back in the day when home satellite dishes were the size found on military installations. Looked to me like an easy transition from lugging hardware and software around suburban backyards to checking in campground guests and leading cave tours. I can only imagine what the side of his next truck might look like.

The fishing was subpar even for this time of year. I spent a day over on the Fishing Creek in Clinton County, where I caught a few small brookies in the morning before an all-day rain finished the expedition. Another day on the Elk yielded only a small brownie. A decent caddis hatch that evening on the Penns Creek brought up several large fish, but all I could manage was one hook-up that lasted all of fifteen seconds. My last day was spent on another section of the Penns under a beautiful, clear sky, smelling the wildflowers and contemplating the universe—a fishless day, but utterly enjoyable. On my way back to the campground, the weather report jarred across the constant static of the van radio, announcing the arrival of a wicked Canadian air mass that would drop the night temperatures to freezing. I wasn't up for a night of discomfort, so I went over to Pete, who was about to lead the last tour of the day into the cave and inquired about a cabin. He gave me the one closest to the cave's entrance.

I disassembled my campsite and moved my essentials to the cabin in the early evening before one last try on the Penns. The swiftly moving cold front cut my fishing short, swirling winds slapping branches against each other in a fury of cracks and pops. Hurriedly, I packed up my gear and tossed everything in the back of the van. Tilting and rocking along the uneven surface, I spurted back up Pine Creek Road. In the short span of twenty minutes, the front passed. When I returned, the campground was eerily quiet. The night chill moved the RVers into their trailers. The campground help was gone for the evening, and God knows where Pete was, if he even spent his nights at the place. I made dinner and broke open a seltzer water and sipped a drink while staring at the moths skating on the cabin's kitchen window. I mulled over a depression I had struggled with in therapy earlier in the year. Outside of fishing, these had been difficult times for me. After twenty-three years, my career of choice was feeling uninspiring, confining, yet I was afraid of making a change, not wanting to start over at midlife, yet knowing I could not go on. I mulled over my marriage and the lack of passion my partner and I experienced and began to wonder if I made the right choice twenty years earlier. I wanted badly not to stay stuck in this web of dissatisfaction, pondering the source of these woes and how immobilized I felt. It was mostly fear, I decided. I was fearful of taking risks with myself—my feelings, my relationships, my career. I wasn't sure what exactly I was afraid of, but it was all encompassing, like being wrapped in a thin filament of gauze that allows you to see but stifles any attempt to move. I knew I needed to descend deep into my soul to shred the fabric of those fears if I was to break the hold they had on me.

Grabbing a penlight while throwing a sweater over my head, I walked out into the frosty, starlit night over to the entrance to the cave. There was a wrought-iron gate the size of a garage door closed in front of it. A latch was clamped over a bar, but surprisingly there was no lock on it. I pulled the cold metal toward me and the gate groaned as it opened. The penlight barely illuminated the cobblestone entrance into the cave. A bat whisked by me, so close to my face that I could feel the faint stir of air from its wings. I ambled into the first room of the cave, the place where the tourists gather to hear Pete's rendition of the cave's geologic history. Something about limestone substrates being dissolved by underground streams during the Pleistocene epoch. That night I didn't care how it got there or how old it was. For me, the cave's attraction was mystical, a place where immersion of the psyche became necessary, as if I had no choice over its plea. I meandered into the next room, a good fifty feet from the entrance, where the stalactites spit droplets on to the cave floor in a monotonous drone. Several more bats angled swiftly past me. I directed the light in search of the cave's innards, locating the path toward the cave's largest rooms. Rising gently up an incline, the third room of the cave enveloped me. At that point,

I turned off the light and put it in my pocket. The cold stillness was interrupted only by the droplets and the occasional passing of bats. I inched my way up the incline without the light. I could see nothing. With my eyes wide open, the blackness revealed the entrance to a stark, featureless infinity. Undaunted, I felt confident as I made my way into what appeared to be the center of the dark, empty space of chilled, dank nothingness. Finally, I stood motionless for a very long time, feeling calm, serene actually. It seemed like what must be the very moment before death—alone, black, damp, with barely a discernible sound. And no need to be afraid.

11

Drought Fishing

Though Bob is one of my closest lifelong friends, he is not a seriously addicted fly-fisherman. He throws a nice line with a decent graphite rod that I gave him a few years back for some work that he did for me, but he'd be just as happy casting spoons or crankbaits at bass or pike. He's always fervently plying the fly rod when we're together, even though we have this understanding that he can fish any way he wants. Our fishing excursions fulfill a need other than honing our fishing skills, though. They're more a vehicle for sustaining a deep friendship that has held together through each of our marriages, raising kids, and bumpy rides through our respective careers.

Bob and I spent a day and a half together up on the East Branch of the Delaware before our friend Henry joined us, setting up the camp, attempting a few stretches of river, and catching up on each other's news. We lived apart at that time, he in Massachusetts and I in Pennsylvania. We met when we both worked together in Philadelphia. When Henry linked up with us, we had decided that it was important to crank up the male bonding mode. I used to think that true friendship was the non-judgmental acceptance of your neuroses by the other person. Now

I've come to realize that making total fun of those neuroses is what it's all about. This type of camaraderie highlights the fact that others fail to take you as seriously as you take yourself, and sometimes you need that reminder to gain a fresh perspective. Or just meet to solve the world's problems which is what we did as well. Hell, we had to on that trip. The fishing was terrible. The region was succumbing to a prolonged scarcity of rain. Rivers were down and the heat index suggested that roasting potatoes on the sidewalk was a better use of your idle time.

We did attempt to meet an evening hatch where the Beaverkill greets the East Branch. Surprisingly, there was one, and small wild rainbows were rising all around us, mostly taking emergers. I suspected something unusual though. Many of the fish were flopping completely out of the water. This was characteristic behavior for a seldom-encountered hatch that has always baffled me when I come across it. "Black caddis," I yelled to Bob. Of course, neither of us had the fly. The dries aren't particularly effective anyway because the insect bounds out of the water and hyperventilates about fifteen inches above it, bouncing up and down like a dribbling basketball, driving the fish absolutely crazy. The best I could do was a few refusals on a slate-gray emerger, while Bob flogged the water endlessly. Henry slashed spoons for a few minutes before declaring, "They're teasing us."

The next day was as hot and sultry as the previous two, so hanging around the campground was a better alternative than trying to fish. We visited our neighbors, a couple of guys from Jersey who fished bait exclusively on the Pepacton Reservoir. They didn't catch lots of fish, but one guy got a five-pound brown early in the morning. Henry took mental notes. Without actually saying it, I think he was making analogies to charter boat fishing. When we left them, he turned to me as if to focus on the key detail of the exchange. "Sawbellies...remember that."

That evening, as we were about to consider which section of the river to fish, I felt on edge. The action was slow. Of the three of us, I'm the dedicated fly-fisher. I mean, I'll go anytime, anywhere. But the drought conditions even had me considering other options. After dinner, we were sitting at the picnic table. I stared at both of them mischievously.

"Whadda you say we go to a topless bar tonight instead of fishing?"

"Where?" Henry shot back.

"Monticello. I made a wrong turn and headed past the racetrack. There's a strip joint just up the road from the track."

"How long to get there?"

"Less than an hour," I offered.

"I'm in," Henry countered.

Bob was a bit more skeptical, sour actually, but we finally got him to agree.

Monticello, it seems, was created when God thought that urban blight should not be confined to cities and decided to locate some at the foot of the Catskills next to a busy freeway. Most people heading for the outdoor recreation destinations of the Catskills aren't even aware it exists, except as an exit sign on the New York State Thruway. It's part of the Borscht Belt, not far from the major entertainment hotels where people from New York used to go for the illusion of getting away to the country. On the west side of town is the "business route," where the tacky bars and strip joints usher your way to the racetrack. To an outsider like me, the whole place seemed like a kind of repository for lost souls. But hey, this is no knock on that, for we were aiming to become lost too. The woeful fishing forced us into this desperation.

The drive down to Monticello was forty-five minutes of silence punctuated by muted sighs and barely audible fragments of conversation. It seems we were all catching Bob's moody demeanor. We headed straight for the track as a warmup diversion until our real intentions could surface. When we pulled into the darkened, empty parking lot it became immediately obvious that there was no racing on Monday nights.

"Okay, let's go to the bar," Henry interjected, breaking the silence while steering his truck around a dumpster. "Where is it?"

"Turn around and head up the road a half-mile," I directed. "It's on your left."

We drove back toward town and came upon a dimly lit parking lot with one of those portable signs with only a few bulbs left in it, announcing in black, plastic letters against a yellow background, "featuring AMBER, TIFFANY, and DESIREE." Everybody knows what they are featuring. I envisioned legs as long as your trout (or maybe Gierach's trout anyway). For some strange reason, the nearly empty parking lot didn't dampen our ambitions. We burst through the front door and the place was conspicuously quiet. The stage for Amber and her friends appeared desolate, looking like a tiny actors guild theater long after the play has ended. We were, in fact, the only ones in the place. As we strode up to the bar, an attractive barmaid approached, noticing our expectant glances shifting to curious gazes toward the dark corners.

"Can I help you boys with anything?"

"We're looking for a little trouble," I sharply replied.

"There's none here tonight. The girls are off on Mondays."

Made sense. No racing, no bar fun. Our disappointment turned to full-blown depression. The girlie show was as bad as the fishing. There'd be no hatch tonight for fly-fishing cowboys. I guess Amber, Tiffany, and Desirée needed a night off too. We fought off the boredom with a few rounds of pool. The night ended thirty-five minutes later when I threw myself in front of the cigarette machine to save Bob from buying his first pack in fifteen years. Acts of friendship display themselves under strange circumstances sometimes. We headed back to Downsville (no irony intended), our shallow desires thwarted by the bleak conditions and cheap beer. Bob, I think, was silently grateful.

The hefty brown thrashes at the end of the thick, nylon fishing line, bending the fiberglass rod to near breaking. After many crosses out to the open water, the weary fish finally relents and comes toward the beach. A few more turns of the clunky spinning reel lead the trout into shore. I hurry to the water's edge, slipping on the loose gravel as I excitedly hoist the brawny fish out of the water. Surely, it's a seven-pounder, the largest trout I've ever caught. Do I keep it? Do I get it stuffed? Can you proudly display a monster trout over the fireplace caught on a piece of equipment that rightfully belongs on the back of a tow truck? What do you tell the folks admiring the embalmed ornament, with fly rod leaning suggestively over in the corner? Ethical dilemmas...do I need to be dealing with them now, on a fishing trip? Good God, what if I catch another? A nine-pounder...!

"Hey Lou! Hey, wake up!"

I heard a rapping on my van and peered out into the misty shroud. Bob was staring at me on the other side of the glass with a warped grin, like a punitive teacher who takes pleasure in disciplining his students. It was five in the morning, time to commit a personal heresy. I rubbed my eyes and wondered if my dream would turn into some kind of pained reality. I brought three fly rods along for the trip, but a fall from grace is when you have to borrow a stump puller for a descent into the nether world. I fumbled to put on some clothes and flopped out of my van to get some coffee. Bob handed me a cup and pointed to a fiberglass spin outfit leaning against a fat maple. I looked it over, taking in the sordid details. Open face, discount store reel, twelve-pound test nylon curling through the eyes of the cream-colored rod. It looked frighteningly familiar. It'd been years since I'd used one. Seems that no matter what I fished for these days I use a fly rod. Even carp. I went over to the tree and picked it up and shook it a few times, as if judging its action would make its use any more palatable. I packed a six weight with some streamers and woolly buggers, just in case. Hoping for the same success as our neighbors, the three of us made a pact to go to the reservoir this morning for a shot at those huge browns that roam the opaque water in the deep drop-offs near shore. In a half-hour, we find ourselves groveling near the minnow tanks at the local bait shop.

"We'll take two dozen sawbellies," I said to the clerk as I sauntered up to the counter, as if I had done this sort of thing on a regular basis.

"Don't have any. We'll get another batch on Thursday."

The three of us looked at each other with some misgiving.

"Well, what else do you have?" I asked.

"Herring."

"Are they any good for the big browns?" I inquire foolishly, the clerk knowing that this sucker was born one minute ago.

"Yeah, terrific," he replies in almost deadpan fashion.

"Good, then give us some."

"Twenty-four?"

"Yeah."

The clerk looks at us skeptically, then grabs a net and heads for the tanks.

"What else do we need to fish the reservoir?" Henry interjects, not wanting to leave anything to guesswork.

"You'll need permits," the clerk fires back.

"Got any?" Henry asks.

"No, you get them at the water authority office, across the road. They open at eight."

"How much are they?" I inquire.

"The permits are free, but it costs $3.50 to get your picture taken." We gave each other furtive glances, knowing that we'd probably be bending the rules a bit if we had to. Hell, the fishing might be over by eight.

"Where's your bucket, bub?" the clerk snorts as he looks at me.

"Uh... yeah...you got any?" I stammer, totally blowing my cover by this point.

"The Styrofoam ones at the end of the aisle are a buck-fifty-nine." It's obvious this clerk has seen the likes of us before, so he doesn't bother trying to sell the primo units with aerator and oxygen tablets. The street urchins tumbled into town for a day, and he knows it. We leave the store and head for my van. Henry looks at Bob, then me, and pronounces the obvious: "We'll get the permits later...if the fish are biting."

The curvy drive along the south shore of the Pepacton Reservoir brought on momentary introspection. Looking down toward the water, I gazed where the riverbed once coursed, imagining it hiding plunges and bend pools, riffles, and moist, fern-laced seeps. They were places where anglers enjoyed the surroundings as much as the fishing. I never much liked the idea of creating a man-made lake if you had to block the flow of a perfectly respectable river. The East Branch of the Delaware, from reports that I've seen, was a mighty fine brook trout stream, as it flowed through the hemlock ridges just east of Downsville. The dam was built before the environmental conscience of the nation took hold, when lament was a more abundant reaction than outrage. Full-frontal assault on a trout stream is a little more difficult these days. Yet, it's a quiet morning, and the sun squinting over the haze-covered hilltops on to the still water had a pleasing effect. We found a desolate finger of the lake at the east end and spilled out of the van to assess a likely shoreline refuge. We set up shop along a steep gravel bank exposed by the prolonged dry spell, spreading apart to give ourselves just enough space to recognize the mutual respect that bait fishers have for each other. It's a different code than fly-fishing, but there's still a code. Henry took the left side; Bob seized a wide space in the middle and immediately began casting a large spoon thirty yards out. I positioned myself on a boulder to the right. My stubby rod had a size eight hook and some lead already attached. It was time for a necessary ritual. Reaching into the bait container, I grasped a herring and held it up to the morning light. It was a smallish fish, about three inches in length, with a dark green back and silver sides, with a sharp hint of blue becoming obvious when you turned it a certain way. I stared into his tiny, glass-like eye. I could sense the fear in the slippery, quaking fish as I inspected his fragile mouth. I rotated my wrist and exposed his back to the point of the hook. A sense of fatalism came over me. I felt numb and indifferent. After piercing the hook in his back, I rinsed my hand in the bucket around his skittish cousins and prepared to cast. The terminal rig flipped over itself as it traveled about thirty feet. The lead and minnow diced the surface of the still lake simultaneously, sending sharp ripples in every direction. I turned to Henry and Bob and gave them a satisfied grin. Bob was still splashing lures, while Henry shifted his weight on the round stone he sat upon. This was serious engagement, so no one spoke. It was time to stare intently at the line in front of you and monitor for the vicious strike we had come to expect, and rather soon, I might add.

The sun was cutting through the morning film. Bob had abandoned casting lures and switched to a herring rig. Each of us glanced at the other's line every minute or so, trying to anticipate who was going to tie into one and ignite the competitive juices of the other two. There was a lot of manufactured glory riding on the next fish. Well beyond our lines, a large fish broke the surface. Perhaps a feeding frenzy was about to start? We were hopeful. Two minutes later, another violent splash rocked the still lake, this time to our right. And we waited. We waited some more. The sun shifted higher, burning off all the mist. A breeze stirred, causing the surface to ripple slightly. No more activity occurred on the lake for another twenty minutes, yet we were each poised by our respective rods.

I realized the problem with waiting is that when you forget your thought repellent, your mental motor starts interfering with your mission. I glanced down at the stump puller, then over at my rod tube resting on the gravel, containing my six weight. Distinct, disturbing rumblings began escaping from my other self. The trouble with slinging hardware or bait was that it has no soul. I nominated—no, appointed—a frightful herring to do my bidding for me. Slinging a tangled rig of lead and leader off a rocky shoreline hardly required any measure of self. I'd become a victim of fishing, allowing it to prevail over me rather than taking my fate into my own hands. I felt I was performing a bloodthirsty ritual that lost its meaning when we began to fish for sport as opposed to our own survival. This type of fishing was not a search for answers or redemption. It never begged the question: why? You've already known, and the answer is never pretty. The fly rod at least had a certain dignity. I transitioned.

Near the end, Bob had a few follows by small fish when he changed back to a spoon. Henry called it quits, thrusting his rod down in disgust. I made a few more casts, bereft of fish or even interest in a streamer. The rest of the herring were liberated. We agreed to reinvest the money for the permit photos in breakfast at the local diner. While there, Henry and Bob plotted a canoe trip for the afternoon. Poking at some French toast, I felt bemused by the contradictions. I left my soul to trout fishing's pawn broker, while poaching in the birthplace of American fly-fishing. Then I tried to claim it back by laying fly line over an artificial impoundment that trapped and buried some of the most pristine and sacred waters in the Catskills. It's a strange, unfamiliar path that we've sometimes taken to retrieve a troubled spirit, but who's to judge lost souls. I never viewed fly-fishing as anything more than a refuge from the toils of economic necessity, but I'm beginning to reconsider that now. From the diner's window, I saw the dust from the gravel parking lot settling on the pickups and cars. Another cloudless sky hovered over another fishless day. No one knew when it might rain again.

12

Perkiomen Nightmares

Perkiomen is of Lenni Lenape origin, meaning "place where cran-
berries grow." The Perkiomen Creek rises off South Mountain, not too
far from Allentown, and flows south for about ten miles before it enters
the Green Lane Reservoir. About six miles downstream from the source,
it is joined by the Hosensack Creek, near the village of Palm. Those first
few miles of the Perkiomen are considered Class A wild trout waters by
the Pennsylvania Fish Commission, meaning there is sufficient density
of fish in a defined area to meet that criteria. It is a small headwater
stream in that section, lined with thick brush, making fly-fishing a near
impossibility except in a few locations. There are mostly wild browns
with a few remnant brookies populating some tiny tributaries. Except
for the brookies, the fish are originally from hatchery stock that managed to migrate over the years to the colder, more remote water and
began to reproduce. After the creek flows through the wooded hills, it
passes through roughly three miles of pasture before entering a marshy,
tree-lined lowland near the junction with the Hosensack Creek. There,
it gets another flush of cooling water, lifting the capacity for holding
a few wild fish, for the next two miles. At the East Greenville Water

Authority intake, a diversion siphons off some of the stream for the town's secondary drinking water supply. Below the intake, the occasional wild trout can be found seasonally in spring where the stream eventually flows into the Green Lane Reservoir. Though it is popular in the early season and has some decent hatches, the last four miles before the reservoir typically warms too quickly after May to support trout. Some anglers used to think that the stocked fish migrated to the reservoir to live, but studies show that the oxygen level below the cold-water thermocline is too low to support a trout population.

This is a portion of southeastern Pennsylvania where the last of the rural farms are being penned in on three sides by development pressure. Cash-poor, land-rich farmers ply this area with mostly dairy farms, though a couple of beef and hay operations hold on as well. It is decidedly rural and conservative. Many of the farms have been passed on from family to family over the generations. But farming small acreages does not pay a lot, so there is considerable enticement to sell. This region is a little over fifty miles from the center of Philadelphia, so urban sprawl is a short drive away from the last rural vestiges of a life more remembered than lived for a lot of folks in the neighboring communities. Bulldozers have a way of slicing right through the heart of the last best places.

*   *   *   *   *   *   *   *

Toward the end of my weekly forays to the Tulpehocken, I became more curious about Trout Unlimited (TU) since I had heard several anglers refer to it and one pointedly asked me if I "belonged to the club." My thirst for learning how to catch trout on a fly began in earnest in the mid-1980s (the days before cell phones, the internet, and micro-breweries), so one day I found myself in the magazine section of the local pharmacy and *Trout* magazine jumped out at me. I bought the issue and subsequently subscribed. Next thing I know, I was getting patches, bumper stickers, and congratulatory letters. That's when I knew that this was no ordinary magazine subscription. (Note: TU for quite some time has not offered issues for sale to the general public.)

My view of trout anglers garnered from *Trout* magazine and pictures in the state council's newsletter was that these folks were a band of demented rock throwers and boulder pushers, something I had a hard time snuggling up to. But I had an intuitive sense that these were also deeply passionate fishermen, and I could relate to that. It looked like they were trying to save local fishing, or in some cases even make it better. The trouble was my local chapter, Perkiomen Valley, was in a coma. To make a long story short, I ended up with a mailing list that led to revitalizing the chapter. It was a very naïve move at the time. It seems that anyone dim-witted enough to call a meeting deserved to be president, which became my karmic fate. Fumbling along at first, doing one of those "values clarification" exercises so popular with human resources types, it soon became evident why the chapter needed to exist and why it was important. Within the first month of the chapter's rebirth, a nasty agricultural run-off poisoned a mess of trout on the Hosensack Creek. I followed up with multiple calls to the Pennsylvania Department of Environmental Protection on that, pushing for fines and public shaming of the offender, to the point where the state employee on the other end of the line essentially chastised me with a don't-call-us-we'll-call-you response. It was my introduction to the world of environmental protection.

*　　　*　　　*　　　*　　　*　　　*　　　*

At about the same time that I resurrected the chapter, a legal settlement was reached between a regional environmental defense agency and an industrial production facility, one of the largest employers in the

Upper Perkiomen Valley. The company was found liable for significant pollution violations of the Perkiomen Creek during the 1980s. With the six-figure fine in the neighborhood of $200,000 that was imposed on them, the settlement called for the company to pay for a study that would lead to identification of the current pollution problems on the Perkiomen and a management plan to address them. The organization chosen to conduct the study was the Delaware Riverkeeper Network, at the time an affiliate of the American Littoral Society. In the first public hearing on the project, the Riverkeeper Network unveiled a consulting agency who would do the water quality study. A consultant got up in front of the audience of about fifty participants and stated that he thought the problems with the Perkiomen were not caused by specific pollution events from a single source, but rather "nonpoint" sources. They were going to do the study to figure out where these nonpoint sources were emanating, what the major pollutants were, and most importantly, who was responsible.

The Perkiomen Chapter of TU (#332) was formed in 1979 by Lee Hartman and other individuals who mostly lived in one of the three boroughs of East Greenville, Pennsburg, or Red Hill, situated in the Upper Perkiomen Valley. By TU standards it was a small chapter with, at most, a dozen active members, judging by the old newsletters I perused as part of the leadership handoff. Among the handful of members involved in the chapter were three notable, passionate fly anglers. Don Douple, who not only was an excellent fisherman but a popular guest speaker at many Pennsylvania TU chapter meetings, advanced angler knowledge through his work in entomology and video captures of in-stream hatch events and fish movements. The aforementioned Lee Hartman became a well-known guide, outfitter, author, and one of the first western explorers of cold-water fisheries in post-Cold War Russia, fishing with luminaries such as Ted Williams (Major League Hall of

Fame member and one of the purist hitters of the game) and basketball coach Bobby Knight. Yaz Yamashita became a precision fly-tier whose realistic imitations captured the fascination of many. He had the honor of contributing a collection of flies housed at the American Museum of Fly-Fishing. He even designed a tool for making extended bodies, a few of which are still floating around in the hands of collectors. The chapter, though small, had a rich history, and its signature project was a platform deflector along the East Greenville Water Authority property built in the days when habitat improvement meant a structure that would improve holding water. It has held up through the years and was still there when I last visited the stream in 2012. As with many small chapters, succession becomes a revolving door and eventually it takes one too many spins and leadership drops off. Fortunately, the treasurer made the necessary filings to the national organization and held on to the pertinent documents to allow resuscitation. With the approval of some of the former board members, I became the proud custodian of a mailing list, checkbooks, receipts, and old newsletters. A board was quickly assembled, and we were officially blessed.

Having spent most of my incipient fly-fishing forays along the Tulpehocken Creek, I knew next to nothing about the Perkiomen Watershed. In the town of Schwenksville where I lived, about ten miles south of the Green Lane Reservoir, the Perkiomen presents as a warm water fishery where the PA Fish and Boat Commission used to stock muskies, but I mostly fished for smallmouth, sunfish, and crappies. The Commission did stock trout in the upper Perkiomen between Tollgate Road and the borough of Red Hill, a distance of about three miles. The County of Montgomery stocked a half-mile section before the creek entered the Green Lane Reservoir and deemed the area Fly-Fishing Only. As is typically the case in southeastern Pennsylvania, stocking occurs in impaired waterways, the places where trout can't reproduce on their own. In fact, most die of suffocation because water temperatures exceed the lethal limit. I suspected that was the case for the upper Perkiomen, but in the spirit of management-by-walking-around, I did a drive along the creek from its lower segment by the reservoir up to the village of Hereford. In my cursory drive around the upper watershed, the impairment was obvious. The absence of trees and shrubs along the riparian buffer was the death sentence for trout. Above Hereford, the topography and foliage changes dramatically from wide floodplain meadows to steep, wooded inclines of second-growth deciduous forest. The floodplain, of course, was ideal for farming and grazing while the steep incline prohibited such land use. The absence of trees and streamside vegetation occurred many generations ago when the upper valley was first settled by Europeans, the descendants of whom populate much of the farming community today. In their ignorance of environmental consequences and their quest for efficiencies, farming and grazing practices decimated the riparian buffer, eventually making it treeless, allowing the banks to erode in storm events, causing excessive silting. Most of this damage was caused by dairy and beef herds grazing the vegetation and trampling the banks. Add to that the defecation problem. The average pastured, 1,200-pound cow produces about 100 pounds of manure per day. If you estimate a seven-month pasture season, that comes to about 10.5 tons of manure per year per cow. With the typical dairy herd at 100 head, you are looking at 10,000 tons of manure deposited in pastures per year. And that is just from one farm. I didn't count the number of farms I passed on that drive, but if you included a couple of tributaries to the Perkiomen, the number of dairy farms totaled about fifteen in the upper valley. That, my friends, comes to quite a load of you-know-what. When it rains, a lot of that you-know-what gets washed into the stream. So when I mentioned earlier that the Green Lane Reservoir had little to no oxygen below the thermocline (about ten feet under the surface) and you understand that eutrophication of stillwater comes from oxygen being consumed by nutrients like those provided by cow manure, you can begin to appreciate the enormity of the problem. But I didn't do all those calculations in my head on that drive. I didn't even know anything about cows. But I could see the lack of trees along the banks of the stream, and intuitively I knew that trees mean shade and shade is cooler than full sun, so if our stocked trout couldn't make it past the middle of June, you could pretty much see why there was an absence of any wild trout.

Now, if people were directly responsible for depositing 10,000 tons of raw manure in a stream from a single source, there would be an outcry of epic proportions, sewage plants costing in the millions would be immediately built, and politicians would be glad-handing at the ribbon-cutting. The problem with cows is they don't have jobs, so they can't be assessed hookup fees to pay for the waste treatment. And farmers, who are cash-poor, can't do it nor do they have the incentive to. So back to the study. After a year's worth of data, which some chapter members including myself helped collect, the conclusion was, well, mystifying. The township below the cow-trodden zone was blamed for the ills of the creek by failing to manage land use correctly. Not only was this an amazing conclusion, but it was an outright misrepresentation of the facts. It angered local officials and was met with skepticism by most rational folk. At the wrap-up meeting after the presentation, I uttered loud enough for most to hear, "$200,000 spent and not one tree planted." The recommendations from the study were largely ignored, and it's now collecting dust. The owner of the reservoir—at that time the Philadelphia Suburban Water Company—commissioned another study, this one costing $125,000. The township wasn't blamed in this one, and non-point pollution from unidentified sources was acknowledged as the chief culprit.

Lessons learned: Local politics rule the day when it comes to assigning blame, and there's real money in consulting, but not a lot in activism.

*   *   *   *   *   *   *

Parallel to these events, our chapter started growing. Folks volunteered for positions on the board including those of Vice President, Treasurer, and Newsletter Editor. Others took undefined roles on the board. We started having successful meetings. We were told by previous board members that to interest the rank-and-file in coming out we had to have programs. Most were about fishing tactics on local or regional streams, offering nominal stipends to local experts in most cases. We even started doing a couple of stream clean-up projects. This was all just nibbling around the conservation edges, but we got a few people beyond the dedicated board members to give up their Saturday mornings to make the Perkiomen a better place—not necessarily for trout, but for fishermen and property owners.

The most valuable program we sponsored at that time cost us a t-shirt. Kristen Travers from the Stroud Water Research Center showed up one evening to give a presentation on riparian buffers. I don't even remember how we got her name. This was in the early 1990s, before the internet became well-established, and her role was in public education for the research center. *Riparian buffer* was not a term thrown around at a lot of Trout Unlimited meetings, or publications for that matter, at that time. Her presentation was profound. Stroud Water Research Center is still located in Avondale, Chester County, Pennsylvania, about fifty-five miles south of our location, along the White Clay Creek. At the time of our connection with them, they were affiliated with the University of Pennsylvania but are now an independent non-profit. Research at the Center revealed much about healthy streams, and Kristen presented succinctly and authoritatively. Those healthy streams had an abundance of native vegetation, largely trees and shrubs, that had two immediate effects: holding the stream banks in place to prevent erosion and shading the water to lower temperature up to ten degrees on the warmest days. Those two facts alone got everybody's attention. Some trees were better than others. In our region the leaf litter of sycamores, red maples, and river birch appeared to produce the highest value detritus. It kind of goes like this: leaves that drop into a stream provide the food sustenance for the larval and nymph stages of aquatic organisms that live in the stream. Leaf matter is lodged in the cobble of a stream where it is readily accessible as a food source for the kind of insects trout anglers like most: mayflies, stoneflies, and caddis flies. That garnered even more attention from the group assembled that night. The size of the riparian buffer mattered a lot in terms of how much pollution and sediment was kept out of streams. Three-hundred feet was the ideal buffer size. Monetarily, a buffer that size could be justified by a selective wood harvest. A smaller buffer size reduced the pollution screening efficiency, but even the smallest buffer provided shade and erosion prevention, two key components that enabled trout habitat as opposed to fallfish habitat. Personally, I had gained more information that night as a fly-fishing conservationist than all the sum total of readings, Earth Days, and conferences I had ever previously encountered. Armed with these facts, the chapter was ready to take on its mission with greater confidence in the outcome it could produce. What we would find out along the way is that applying science to land that you don't own involves a separate daunting set of challenges.

Our chapter, through the efforts of Vic Attardo, our next president in succession and local fish and game columnist, was able to finagle $5,000 from the local state representative from a fund euphemistically known as WAM or Walking Around Money. These are little pet projects that make everybody look good and photo ops are a must. The money was contingent on being used by a farmer to let his pasture be fenced in along the stream, with a couple of cattle crossings thrown in for good measure. Vic located a farmer willing to allow the fencing project, Keith Masemore, an affable fellow who was a supervisor in the adjoining Hereford Township and owner of about 100 head of dairy cattle. His property was located on an unnamed tributary of the Perkiomen whose summer flows were about three cubic feet per second—certainly not a stream anyone would be fly-fishing for trout on anytime soon. One casual leap and you could cross it. That tributary had five consecutive parcels along it, all dedicated to cattle farming (four dairy and one beef), none with exclusionary fencing. Masemore's was the second property down from the forested region that did contain wild trout, albeit a small population by fish commission standards.

With a lot of enthusiasm and an equal amount of ignorance, lack of planning, and financial gymnastics, we proceeded to arrange for a contractor to fence the 1,300-foot stream buffer. The PA Fish and Boat Commission enabled us to install two cattle crossings. Most of this work was contracted, but the crossings required manually installing ballast and stone. Six months later, when one of the crossings washed out, four of us moved many tons of rock and urbanite to hardscape the borders of the crossing so they would not wash out again. Of course, we ran out of money when the crossings needed to be repaired. It was our first time doing this. Like a lot of other first-time experiences, you get better as you do more.

After we finished the project, I went back to the stream. We had basically fenced the cattle away from the tributary. No riparian plantings were made (we had no funds for that). Still, the results were amazing. In that short period of time, grasses grew to two feet tall, overlapping the banks and offering the stream its first shade and sediment barrier in at least 100 years, if not more. The water was much clearer than the cattle-trammeled banks before fencing. Though the buffer was new, it was clear that the science presented by Kristen Travers was actualizing before our very eyes.

Not long after we completed the Masemore project, Keith invited me to his annual open house where he invites neighbors to tour the farm operation. Among the more revealing aspects of this open house are the fact that he lays his tax forms out on the kitchen table for those interested in farm income. That previous year he cleared $4,000 in net profits. Not exactly what you would call a comfortable living, and certainly an eye-opener for anybody who thinks that the simple fix of streambank fencing can be implemented by the landowner on their own on these marginal farms.

Lessons learned: Develop an actual plan and budget. Seek partners who have grant proposal and project management capacity and technical expertise for things like locating a fence line and stream crossings. Have more than four volunteers show up at a project day. Small-scale farmers on the east coast don't have a lot of money to throw at projects like this.

      *   *   *   *   *   *   *

"So, when are you guys going to come down to my place? I'm losing a lot of good soil to the creek." Those were the words Don Bair uttered about a month after we finished the Masemore farm project. He owned a farm a half-mile downstream from the Masemore property along that same unnamed tributary. Don was also a supervisor in Hereford Township and part-time beef producer on about thirty acres of pasture. He took a couple of chapter officers for a tour, me included. Here the stream meandered through meadow and wetlands trodden by twenty head of 1,200-pound Black Herefords. The banks were beat pretty bad, and erosion was taking its toll, not to mention all the cow pies that wash into the stream after a heavy rain.

"Don, we have to find the money first, and we think we have some sources that we could tap. We'll get back to you in the spring." I was not about to let this fish get off, but the truth was we were broke and a bit under-resourced. The stream length in question was about 2,600 feet, twice what we had accomplished at Masemore's farm with the addition of removing invasive multi-flora rose as one of the conditions of a cooperative agreement. We had to put Don off until we could figure out money, logistics, volunteer support, and timing. We had a second willing farmer without having to recruit and sell the conservation benefits, and we were not about to tell him no, especially after we saw how quickly the stream repaired itself once we kept the cattle out. The only money our chapter could obtain was an Embrace-A-Stream grant from TU National. However, this time we secured an able partner, the Schuylkill Riverkeeper, who had access to additional funding and competent field scientists who could guide the restoration process on a professional level. The Schuylkill Riverkeeper was an affiliate of the Delaware Riverkeeper Network based in Bristol, Pennsylvania. They had their own office in St. Peters Village but have since been folded back into the larger organization. Nonetheless, they were a critical first partner for the Perkiomen Valley Chapter of Trout Unlimited. But even with their expertise, the project on the Bair Farm required a small army of volunteers, and it was the chapter that had to recruit them. By this time, I had moved from Chapter President to Volunteer Coordinator, while Chaz Macdonald took over as President. Having not grown up in the Perkiomen Valley and by this time having moved one watershed over to the Manatawny watershed, my securing at least twenty volunteers over six work sessions seemed a daunting task. The chapter had a roster of about 200, but most lived fifteen to twenty miles to the south, and they did not respond to the call for volunteers when we were working the Masemore project. By necessity rather than intention, I became a community organizer. Every chance to recruit a volunteer to remove multiflora rose, plant trees, or install coir log rolls got my attention. I mailed letters to churches, community associations, and local newspapers and posted notices on what were then incipient fly-fishing forums, fly shops, or any other place that would take them. I recruited my own family, none of whom fished at the time. On our first workday I hoped for twenty volunteers. Turns out, we had to send one of the chapter officers for more donuts. Forty volunteers showed up to assist with all the grunt work. What should have taken more than four hours took two-and-a-half. We had the entire gamut of cultural refugees helping the chapter, everybody from vegetarian tree-huggers to fish-kissing fly-rodders to gun totin' deer hunters. Among the attendees was a regional vice-president of the Pennsylvania State Council of Trout Unlimited who drove 200 miles to make the event. Another volunteer from message board recruitment drove sixty-five miles from the state of Delaware. It was the start of the chapter's Golden Era of stream conservation. All the other workdays fleshed out a volunteer crew sufficient for the tasks. The Bair Farm Project finished on-time and under budget. The chapter learned how to pull off a major project with a solid partner, volunteer support, and adequate funding. Most importantly, that September I took a solo tour of the Bair property to view the work after completion. At the upper end of the property, as the stream curves into a small pool about fifteen feet long, I stopped to inspect. Lightly creeping forward to a small mound above the bank, I noticed subtle motion in the pool. At the head of the pool, in the clear glassy water, I spotted the reason why we were engaged in the struggle to provide good habitat. A nine-inch brown trout was effortlessly finning. As I moved closer, I saw the trail of dark spots across his latter line. His beauty and presence brought the joy one would experience welcoming a newborn. As guaranteed in *Field of Dreams*, if you build it, they will come. Just not in large numbers, yet.

There was one challenge left; in a small community, word gets around when good things happen, but you never know how you will be received until it is your turn to sell an idea to a stranger. In our first two projects, the landowners came to us. There were multiple farms along the unnamed tributary and the main branch of the Perkiomen Creek that needed streambank fencing and riparian plantings. It was now time to knock on doors. During this period, I was self-employed operating a small business, so I was familiar with the notion of offering proposals. We treated stream conservation as a business. By the time we were ready to approach our next landowner—a financial advisor who bought a large chunk of property to keep it from being developed—we took on a more professional approach. When I approached Richard Hoffman, he was vaguely familiar with what we were doing, but I explained the benefits to him and offered to give him a written proposal to create a mow line and plant the riparian buffer of a three-quarter-mile segment of the main branch of the Perkiomen on his property known as Lesher Mill. This was an historic mill site that was farmed right to the edge of the stream for hay by a renter farmer. It was the largest property needing restoration along this portion of the watershed. At the same time, the chapter needed to expand its capacity. The Delaware Riverkeeper Network over-extended its reach in terms of projects and could only offer us technical assistance. We had to find a partner who could apply for and administer large grants.

Fifteen miles to the south, the Perkiomen Watershed Conservancy hosted a variety of children's programs for many years. Only recently did they make a stab at stream restoration lower in the valley, with mixed results. Our outreach to them to work in the Upper Perkiomen resonated well. They had paid staff, grant-writing experience, and a willingness to be the project administrator for this and several other projects. They became the critical third piece in our restoration efforts in the Upper Perkiomen Valley. We now had a partner team of grants administrators, on-the-ground technical assistance, and the chapter's role of soliciting landowners and recruiting volunteers. Our chapter went on to complete a total of twelve stream buffer restorations, most involving exclusionary fencing and riparian plantings in the period between 1997 and 2006, covering 14,435 linear feet (almost three miles). In addition, the chapter completed two pond projects where the original ponds were contributing to excessive stream warming. It also joined other partners in a few ancillary projects. For a small chapter with an annual operating budget of $1,000, our accomplishments were big. During this period, the chapter garnered several awards from the PA State Council of TU, including Project of the Year (1998), Website of the Year (twice), and Conservationist of the Year (2004). Thanks to State Council SE Regional VP Joe Mihok, the Perkiomen Valley was paid a visit by Charles Gauvin, the Executive Director of the National TU organization, who took a tour of the projects.

I would be remiss if I did not mention two volunteers by name who impressed me with their commitment. During a break I sat down next to a woman about 50 years old wearing camo pants and a t-shirt. An announcement at her church service brought her to the restoration event. She told me she didn't fish and then she confided to me that she was recovering from cancer and had her last treatment only two weeks earlier. Her name was Linda Roberts. She lived in the local mobile home park and came to several of our project days until she moved to Allentown a year later. After pulling teeth to get some of our passionate fly anglers out to volunteer (one blew me off after only one volunteer stint), I marveled at the dedication of someone like Linda.

The community of fly anglers can get quite snobbish at times. Fortunately, our chapter members recognized that bait-and-lure anglers enjoy wild trout as much as they did and accepted John Costanzo into our fold. At the time, John was a supremely competent bait angler, and brook trout was his specialty. He would bait his hook with a very small segment of earthworm and hook trout in the upper jaw so as not to allow swallowing of the hook. John worked in a factory in Lansdale making components for arcade machines. He was certainly of modest means but a passionate conservationist, unlike some of our more well-heeled fly-rodders. John was a key volunteer for many of our projects, a real unsung contributor.

During this frenetic time of multiple farm projects, the chapter was blessed with a core of devoted board members who not only volunteered to steward the chapter, but were always counted upon when chapter field work was required. They include: Chaz Macdonald, Scott Repa, Steve Scott, Mike Fries, Jack Steel, Dave Herold, Paul Raubertas and Charles Jack. Most rotated through various offices and each had a complementary skill that gave the chapter a synergy greater than the sum of its parts. Without their valuable contributions, the chapter would not have succeeded. Stream restoration is not a one-person enterprise.

Lessons learned: Landowners sign on for a variety of reasons; some wanted to do the right thing, others wanted a tree screen from the highway, and some wanted to protect their cattle from mastitis and hoof diseases. Beef cattle need a minimum of five strands of high-tensile fencing as electrification will sometimes short-out during flood events. Volunteer recognition is important and the chapter did some, but the majority of volunteers are rewarded by the positive results and they can come from more varied backgrounds than you might imagine. Having written proposals and Memoranda of Understanding (MOU) articulated landowners' and restoration partners' roles, responsibilities, and timelines. Conduct the restoration project like a business.

* * * * * * *

"I gift you, Pachwechen." Glenn Wolf, a Lenape descendent who lived in the headwaters of the Perkiomen near Zionsville offered the name, which translates to "meadow stream." Glenn gave a presentation to the chapter on the history of the Lenape in the watershed and the Lehigh Valley. I found him through the Lenape Historical Society Museum of Indian Culture. The chapter's streambank fencing program straddled the main branch of the Perkiomen and two unnamed tributaries. After all that work, we decided that a stream with a name has a better chance of being protected. Being unfamiliar with the naming process, I researched the protocols through the United States Geological Survey (USGS) where names of geographical features are submitted for approval and eventual placement on all official maps. One of the instructions was to ensure that the stream had not been named in the historical past.

The Pennsylvania Historical and Museum Commission sits inside an imposing oval building among the many official state offices in Harrisburg, the state capitol. The Commission is responsible for the collection, conservation, and interpretation of Pennsylvania's historic heritage. It contains over 5 million artifacts, including historical documents, archeological finds, taxidermy specimens of wild animals, geological specimens, and all manner of relics from the past. I was there for maps. Eventually after registering, I was escorted to the map room by a stiff but courteous staff member.

"Mr. Wentz, do you have any pens with you?" he queried.

"Yes, I have one here in my pocket."

"Give me it," he demanded. I surrendered the pen. "Here's two pencils for notes. We don't want any mark-ups on the maps that cannot be removed."

"Got it," I replied.

"Now, what can I get for you?"

"I'm looking for maps of Berks County, from as far back as you can find."

"I will be back shortly." He then pivoted toward the door and quickly paced out of the room.

Sitting there as if waiting for the vice principal to discipline me, I scanned the empty room. In a museum with 5 million artifacts, there were none in that workspace except for a plain, Formica-surfaced desk and a sturdy wooden chair, probably from the 1950s. The wall above me was partitioned with glass that looked on to the registration counter, most likely so staff could keep an eye on occupants, lest they have mischievous intent with valuable documents. The work of many people brought me to this place, a chance to leave a legacy for the TU chapter and everybody involved. The state of Pennsylvania was a very invested partner in our projects through the Department of Environmental Protection (DEP) with grants and site visits, and now in some small way we were inviting the participation of the government of the United States. As a rather ordinary citizen, I felt connected in a very intimate way with institutions of government that I never thought would be part of my residency in civil society.

Moments later, the door abruptly opened and in walked the minder—I mean staff member. Cradled in his arms were three large volumes, map collections from different periods, which he placed on the table in front of me. I was thinking I should reach into my pocket for a tip. His service was efficient, prompt, and with little emotion.

"Mr. Wentz, this is the oldest one I could find. It is from 1789. The next is from 1822. The last is dated 1854. If you want more recent editions, I'm sure I can find them. When you are finished taking notes, leave the maps on the table and return to the registration desk. You can get your pen there." The staff member then promptly left the room.

I begin paging through the maps. Lifting the crusty pages of the oldest one first, I zoomed in on Hereford Township. The little tributaries came up quickly. Then I noticed little black squares, some with names next to them. These were the original homestead farms. They were spread few and far between. Many of them, the actual fieldstone structures, are still standing today in good condition. Some of the occupant's names from the map are recognizable today as villages or roads. Neither of the streams had names attached to them. I set that map aside and pulled up the one from 1822. There were more dots and a few more geographic features indicated. *Perkiomen* was clearly marked along the main branch, draining the South Hills as it makes its way into Montgomery County near the village of Palm. Again, neither tributary was named. I had my doubts that the 1854 map would turn up anything, but to my surprise, the tributary that parallels the current Route 100 was named *Valley Run*. I don't think I or anyone else had any inkling the stream had a name 100 or more years ago, but somehow it got lost in time. I asked the staff at the desk for a photocopy and they pleasantly obliged. I then exchanged their two pencils for my pen and drove the seventy-five miles back to Pike Township, my residence at the time.

A month later, with my documentation in hand and letters of support from Hereford Township, Washington Township (the origin of Valley Run), and the Lenape Museum of Indian Culture, I submitted the names *Pachwechen Run* and *Valley Run* to be the official names of the tributaries the TU chapter worked so hard on for so many years. About four months later, I received a request for an additional letter of support from the Berks County Commissioners. The commissioners never responded. I anticipated it would hold up the submission. But unexpectedly, three months after that, I received the official document of recognition of the submission of the two names from the US Geological Survey. It was one of my proudest moments in my association with the chapter.

* * * * * * *

I would be lying if I told you the chapter's efforts yielded all rainbows and unicorns. After most of the farm projects were completed, one of the chapter board members got an email from an acquaintance who commutes south on Route 100, which parallels the Class A Wild Trout water in the upper reaches of the main stem above the dairy farms. His cryptic note was something to the effect of, "I thought Class A water was supposed to be free of pollutants. The stream looks like liquid mud." That was a pretty ominous note about the best section of the Perkiomen Creek. Chaz Macdonald and I took a ride up that way. We were informed ahead of time that there was a construction site of high-end homes being built on an old orchard that occupied a steep hill aside the creek. It turns out that working orchards of the 1950s and '60s used pesticides containing arsenic. That arsenic remained in the leaves of the fruit trees, and every year as the leaves fell, they decomposed and the arsenic became part of the soil. The orchard was abandoned as a working farm, and an enterprising developer bought it for luxury home sites. This valley has become the nexus of development pressure. It is the exurbs of both Philadelphia and Allentown. Bucolic hillsides and streamside property are the want of many of the more affluent. It was only a matter of time.

The mitigation of arsenic contamination revolves around soil aeration. On this hillside, giant machines were churning the soil down to several feet deep. In the process, they were disturbing the natural per-colation of groundwater from rain and snow. Neighbors below the hill had springs and rivulets in their yards where none were before, some passing through gardens or front lawns. Without trees or vegetation, loose soil washed heavily into the creek after every rain, no matter how light. The Class A trout water was being ruined before our very eyes. The worst effects were on the property of Ed and Winnie Jensen. Their house was directly below the hillside where the earth disturbance was the most prominent. When we were introduced to them, they told us of instances where their wellhead was submerged in mud, ruining the pump. Mud deposits were a common occurrence on wide expanses of their property. The most disturbing part of this story is the Soil Conservation District of Lehigh County had approved this remedia-tion. They seemed to have the developer's interests at heart, not that of the creek or the neighbors. In this portion of Pennsylvania, the DEP delegates soil and sediment control to the conservation districts, so they had a hands-off policy with respect to these concerns. In my estimation, the district had limited resources and inadequate, inexperienced staff to monitor and intervene in the situation.

The worst pollution event I ever witnessed in my life occurred when myself and a member of the Perkiomen Watershed Conservancy visited the Jensens to discuss a possible restoration on their property. The Jensens were mowing and removing vegetation too close to the stream. Much of it was multi-flora rose, a noxious shrub that can over-take abandoned lots and fields. The thorns are sharp and plentiful. I have punctured many a set of waders trying to access good water buffered by large hedgerows of the plant. It's understandable that someone would want to rid their property of it. In the middle of our discussions with the Jensens, a thunderstorm started brewing to the west. Gloomy, mois-ture-laden clouds stalled above us. Then, without hesitation, buckets of rain started crashing out of the skies. Within minutes, we got to witness what the Jensens and their neighbors has been putting up with for months. Sheets of mud started pouring down the hill, rafting off the road and on to the Jensen property. Standing on their covered balcony, we watched in horror. Ed quickly dashed into the house to get his video camera and began taking footage, adding to the library of environmental insults they had been recording for the purposes of legal action. While he was filming, I was getting silently enraged and spewed a bristled quip to him. "Ed, I don't know how you can remain so calm. I'd be at the Uzi shop by now."

The rain let up but never stopped. Kelly, the staff member from Perkiomen Watershed Conservancy, and I decided further discussion was not productive at the time and decided to leave. We sloshed our way to the cars. I told the Jensens I would be in touch. I was shaken beyond words. As I pulled out of their drive and approached the bridge to the main road, I paused. A wall of sloppy, muddy water rushed under the bridge, raising the level of the creek about three feet in one instant. The side of the hill collapsed 150 yards upstream. It looked like those California mudslides that you see every so often on the news. I became heartbroken beyond anything I had ever felt. All the work on the stream sections and tributaries appeared to be wasted effort. A muddy, soulless creek sluiced through it.

When I got back in touch with the Jensens, I told them it was last-ditch effort time. Winnie Jensen made copies of the video tapes to accompany a scathing letter I wrote to the State Secretary of the DEP, Kathleen McGinty. I also sent the letter to every legitimate news organization in the region and the two water supply companies tapping the Perkiomen Creek farther down the watershed. The news organizations ignored the release, but the water companies tested their supplies for arsenic. Fortunately, none was found. Within a couple of weeks, I was informed that the DEP was assigning their regional staff to investigate the situation. The DEP officials eventually held a public meeting to a packed hall at a local township. I was asked to testify and though a bit lengthy, I made two points to them. The pictures and videos they received as evidence were the finest examples of environmental pornography they would ever get their hands on. Second, though the DEP in another division had been a wonderful grants partner, this lack of oversight was a stab in the back to me and all those who dedicated volunteer time to improve the watershed.

The aftermath was anti-climactic: In the end, the DEP forced the developer to implement an expensive underground filtration system. The creek ran clear again, and the trout population eventually recovered. By this time, I was exhausted, and could no longer contribute. When the next chapter meeting was held, I resigned my post and withdrew from all chapter activities. My environmental activism had to be put on pause. It would take a stronger man than I to continue on. I left everything on the field. No shame in that.

*   *   *   *   *   *   *

August 13, 2011

Before the farm restoration work, the stream temperatures in the lower portion of the Perkiomen before it enters the Green Lane Reservoir were always too warm to hold trout in the summer months of July and August. Even though Montgomery County stocked this fly-only section with trout in the spring, they could not survive the sweltering heat of summer when stream temperatures rose to the lower-and mid-80s. It was considered bass, panfish, and carp water at that time of year. The riparian buffer planted in the early aughts offered some relief, keeping the high temperatures up to around 80 in this section, still too warm for trout but some improvement over past summers. When I left the chapter in 2006, there were four landowners the chapter was not able to recruit. They owned key segments that were not able to be cooled with riparian plantings. If we could have improved those sections, there would have been wild trout habitat from the highlands where the Class A water persisted all the way to the mouth of the reservoir.

The summer of 2011 was particularly wet and cool. On a whim, I decided to check the fishing in the Fly-Fishing Only lower section to see if perhaps a holdover stocked trout may have survived. This section of the stream flows through a low, flat flood plain before entering the reservoir. For years, it had been a hay field planted right to the edge of the banks. Shade was absent and one pool below the bridge crossing the stream at Church Road was euphemistically called "The Erosion Pool." A little after the Perkiomen Valley TU Chapter completed most of its farm projects, the Perkiomen Watershed Conservancy and the Delaware Riverkeeper Network teamed up with the Philadelphia Suburban Water Company (now Aqua Pennsylvania), owners of the reservoir, to implement an impressive riparian planting. Within five years, a great number of sycamores took hold on both banks, along with other native shrubs like silky dogwood and arrowwood. The erosion pool disappeared, becoming a short glide and riffle sequence shrouded in vegetation. In a small amount of time, this section drastically changed.

That morning started cool for August, with a mix of clouds and sun. No other cars were parked along the road. I would have solitude and perhaps catch a nice smallmouth or two, or even more unlikely, a holdover stocked trout. After donning my waders, I decided to make my way downstream toward the mouth of the reservoir. There were a couple of deep pools in that lower section that should contain a few sturdy fish. As I approached the first big pool, I noted that the silver maple hugging the bank stretched its lower branches wide across the stream. After taking the water temperature (66 degrees) and watching the water for a bit, I started to notice some splashy rises. These were not the riseforms of small chubs or dace but more substantial surface breaks. They almost appeared to be the rises of trout chasing small caddis. I decided to circle to the lower end of the pool. Wading carefully, I moved within about thirty feet of the working fish. There may have been eight of them. Tying on a small caddis dry, I got a good drift and an immediate take. The fish tugged, twisted, and turned a few times before coming off. Certainly not a sunfish. Perhaps a small bass, but a tantalizing moment. After letting the water settle, the fish became busy again. Another good drift and another hungry take. The fish struggled heroically but eventually came to hand. It was a magnificent, eight-inch wild brown trout. Magnificent because of its beauty, parr marks trailing down its sides, and mostly because he was there, in water that should not carry a two-year-old, cold-water species, not in any time I or anyone I knew ever fished there in August. Grinning to myself, I released the fish and paused until more surface activity resumed. Fishing for about three hours, I caught seven brownies, all in the eight-to nine-inch range. It was an outlier year to be sure, but it proved the hypothesis that if there was enough shade, the cool water would hold trout year-round. It was gratifying to know that the Perkiomen was almost a trout stream from source to the reservoir.

*　　　*　　　*　　　*　　　*　　　*　　　*

October 21, 2020

It has been a little over eight years since I last visited the Perkiomen Valley. On this day, an array of cosmic motions has landed me back in my former home waters, the place where I, along with the many hardworking members of the Perkiomen Valley Chapter of Trout Unlimited, logged many volunteer hours planting trees, removing nonnative multi-flora rose, and stringing or repairing cattle fencing in the hopes of reviving a stream that wants to hold trout year-round. While it is overcast, no rain is on the horizon. Autumn is at its peak, the leaves flush with color—rusty reds, bright, screaming yellows, tinges of green, even some streaks of purple burst through. With virtually no wind, I decide it is a good day to fish, but first I take a tour of the farms where our restoration work took place. When I moved away, the trees were still mostly saplings, the tallest perhaps eight or nine feet, not offering much in the way of shade as they were just getting established. I did not know what to expect eight years later, but to my great surprise, most attained a height of at least twenty feet, with some up to twenty-five feet, offering a full canopy across the stretches where they were planted. It also appeared that of the hundreds of trees we planted, we maybe lost one or two. Understory, which crept back on its own, looked healthy as well. The only regret I had was it was not mid-summer, so I could not compare stream temperatures to our previous recordings. I then drove upstream along Route 100 and came upon some surprising views. Two of the farm properties that refused our offer of restoration services had abandoned dairy farming. The riparian buffer on one was nearly identical to the restoration sites, indicating that that farm had been out of service for several years, while the other meadow looked to be abandoned within the past year. I could not tell you if dairy prices or retirement precipitated these events, though I have read that milk prices have fallen precipitously. The cautionary tale for dairy farmers according to the article was "get big or get out." The small dairy operations in the Perkiomen Valley cannot afford to get big. The economics of the industry are not good for farmers, but they are good for the stream. Unless there are new encroachments from development to the riparian areas on these meadows, it is likely that the Class A waters will extend down the valley to the farm meadows we restored. That would be a triumph of immeasurable proportions if it occurs. We certainly did our part to make it happen.

The real test, though, is dropping flies in the water, to see if trout recovery really does happen on a serious scale. I was a little less optimistic about the fishing, though. The area received practically no rain in the past two months. Water levels were as low as I had ever seen them. Pools were crystal clear and empty of any signs of life, not only of trout, but minnows, shiners, and dace as well. Nonetheless, I wandered over to Lesher Mill, site of one of the longest stretches of restoration, nearly 3,000 feet. Before and right after the plantings, the fishing in late September or early October usually turned up fallfish, what I like to think of as the eastern version of whitefish, with the big difference being that they usually indicate impaired (read: warm) water. So my expectations were the same: fallfish would likely be the catch of the day.

Tree and shrub plantings change a stream in ways that you might not imagine when you first install native vegetation. The Perkiomen in this stretch became tighter, narrower, more like a small stream than a mid-size stream. The trees were all healthy, of course, and ablaze in color. I pulled out my small stream rod, a seven-foot, six-inch four weight, and attached a tandem of #12 partridge and olive soft hackle wets that I use as searching patterns. Casting in close cover becomes challenging, and as I stepped into the stream twenty feet above the first hole I wanted to fish, my backcast snagged several times. That kind of throws off your rhythm, but after a couple of tries with no success, I moved down to the next pool. On my second cast in that pool, a sloppy affair, I slowly start to strip in my line when a sharp grab tightens the line. In an instant the fish is off. Fallfish? Trout? Something else? After a few more casts, I move downstream about forty yards. This next accessible run used to be a slow-moving pool with steep, eroded, barren banks on its south side. It is now almost completely unrecognizable as it is canopied on both banks. One of the trees was planted so close to the water that it created a root wad undercut by the action of the current. It looks to be a likely lie. I slipped a cast at the head of the root tangle and bang! Fish on. I'm eager to land it, not because it is big (it is not), but because I want to identify the damn thing to satisfy my aching curiosity. After a brief struggle, I grasp the fish in my left hand. A beautiful nine-inch brown trout in fall spawning colors writhes furiously at the end of the tippet. Despite the hatchless conditions and seeming dearth of aquatic insects, the fish appears healthy, wiggling determinedly to escape my grasp. After a few seconds, the fish gets his wish and I get mine—landing an adult trout in what used to be marginal fallfish water. Surely it was a tough day to be on this or any stream. Drought and low water have a way of limiting your chances, but on this day, I realized as I left the colorful canopy of volunteer-planted trees that all our efforts produced a stream profoundly better than we found it. One in which hope has a better chance of becoming destiny.

May 26, 2021

An early heatwave enters the Perkiomen Valley. It is a day I was hoping to see before my move back to Oregon. Official high of 91.4 degrees. I drove around to the locations where Chaz and I took a summer of readings of stream temperatures back in 2004. Today's readings: Peevy Road Bridge, 71 degrees; VFW parking lot, 70.5; lower Lesher Mill, 70; Upper Lesher Mill, 68; Hereford Eco Park, 71; mouth of Pachwechan Run, 70; Pachwechan Run at Tollgate, 72. For comparison, the always cooler West Branch at the Gamelands, 66. Not perfect, but a dozen degrees cooler than the same locations before the stream buffer matured. Water certainly capable of year round trout habitat. The science got it right. Thank you Kristen Travers. You gave us what we needed. Perkiomen Valley TU did the rest, and continues improving the watershed with riparian plantings and instream structures today. Passion and vision has its rewards.

After a cooling thunderstorm, I caught two wild brown trout that evening in what was one of the most temperature and bank degraded pastures before the restorations started. My sojourn back to Pennsylvania was complete, my last curiosity satisfied. Family circumstances have brought me to Oregon, Eugene specifically. Oregon has many big rivers with swift, dangerous currents. I mostly fish the McKenzie and the Willamette for wild rainbow and coastal cutthroat trout. They are beautiful fish, native to the region, and plentiful. Eagle, ospreys, otters, and beavers populate the river valleys here, the mountains are more majestic, and it is home for now, but whenever I go fishing, the riffles and glides of the Perkiomen remain with me on each and every cast.

13

Wild Black Raspberries

I pretty much understand the source of my fishing passion, but have often wondered, like many writers and anglers, why does it persist? Why have I not outgrown a boyhood pleasure that has now become an adult-sized distraction that pervades my life through journeys, conservation projects, and writing? After I examine the quintessential rejoinders about fishing being a vestige of our primal instincts, where one of our forbearers went back to their sustenance stream out of curiosity or pleasure, I search for the core of why I might find myself on streams when I no longer need to be there to survive. The quest for the hidden desire of why I'm attracted to, and in some cases obsessed with, the fishing experience I think dwells closer to how our collective selves function as humans during the times we are away from streams. We tend to be goal oriented in Western civilization. All the discoveries of unique microbiology, new technologies, improved practices in business, medicine, physics, or any other discipline is an expression of our drive toward personal and organizational goals that aim toward a betterment of society and the individual. That is not to say that there aren't some costs associated with these initiatives, and our history is replete with examples. Our historic environmental record comes quickly to mind. We are even driven in our recreation. What probably started out as cultural festivities and games has resulted in an Olympic movement that has individuals endeavoring toward increasingly improbable goals, records that continue to be broken using electronic time pieces that measure in a hundredth of second. Someday, when our speeds and heights have reached a virtual plateau, we will measure successes in one one-thousandth of a second or centimeter, still endeavoring to go faster, jump higher, do better. However paradoxical it may seem at times, sport fishing is often a goal-oriented activity. Most of us would stop fishing if we did not catch fish at least some of the time. Let's face it, if you didn't catch fish, then the germane question would be reduced to *why stand there and cast all day?* Some describe fishing as our only connection with a world closed to us in every other respect, a place of mystery that beckons on one hand yet shrouds its secrets by virtue of its implicit inaccessibility. Then perhaps the goal is not to catch fish for some form of count for competition (though that does seem to be the case for the truly obsessed), but to be intrigued by their presence, which we can do best by holding them in our hand and admiring their beauty or pondering their mystique. Fishing for any species, no matter how low on the value metric, should be all that's necessary for the experience to be complete. But we know it is not.

I assume we fish, in part, to fight, to engage in a struggle. It is our history to be involved in what seems to be a continuous torrent of strenuous efforts. Whether they are political, economic, military, or sporting, participating in intense competition has defined much of our culture. When that ethos is applied to our recreation, particularly fishing, the more vigorous it is the better we like it. Records are kept of the largest fish, the line classes judiciously noted implying that the thinner the line (read: the better, more skilled struggle) the bigger the victory.

And let's face it, fights are about victories. You catch a twenty-two-inch trout and you proudly grunt to yourself "nice fish," implying an outstanding conquest on your part. When a large one bends your rod noticeably and then gets off, there's no shame involved, the fish was just too good for you. We sometimes try to console ourselves with thoughts that it is not the worst thing that could happen, but we always seem to have more clear memories of the one that got away, replaying the struggle in our minds in search of the reason for our failure. Was it a poorly tied knot? Did we fail to inspect the leader for frays after the last snag? Could we have applied too much pressure when the fish turned toward cover during his last run? In effect, we search for personal or equipment improvements that will offer us success the next time. We buy books that describe trout as long as an arm or as fat as footballs. Others plan trips to distant, remote locations where giant trout that have never seen a fly become objects of their giddy determination. Yet all of the focus on struggles and victories with gargantuan trout does not explain the ordinary fishing that most of us do much of the time. The twelve-inch trout gives a good fight, and you are pleased with the results. It's a struggle and a conquest. You've had other and better ones before, but this one is satisfying too. Perhaps then it is the challenge. In a sense, challenges are an extension of our goal-oriented behavior, though we define the terms. *The Guinness Book of Records* is full of challenges that others have defined for themselves, some of them truly inane. We extol oddities like farthest distance traveled by hot air balloon, longest lasting dancing pair, the fastest speed attained by a wind-driven craft on salt flats, as challenges met by determined individuals as if they represented enviable success. We admire individuals who climb rock-faced cliffs as having set the terms and confronted the bold circumstances. Those who sail oceans in diminutive craft are spotlighted on the news. Every day in a thousand ways, individuals set for themselves benchmarks that outline new standards for how to accomplish something that is seemingly beyond reach.

One of the attractions of fly-fishing has to do with the degree of difficulty that the sport offers and the opportunity to prove to ourselves that we are up to the task. Casting technique must be accomplished before you can make any attempt to fish. New knots must be learned while insect types and their respective flies must be identified and matched. Tying flies adds a whole new dimension to the sport. There seems to be an accumulation of knowledge that can never be fully satisfied. Water must be read and rise forms identified. The more you think you know, the more you realize you've just skimmed surface. Even the most accomplished fly-fishers I know admit to being skunked every now and then. And don't think for a minute they aren't ruminating right now about some clue that would have changed the outcome, made the outing a more satisfying event, or even the memory of a lifetime. When we've acquired a certain level of skill, the experience becomes gratifying only because we've set our own terms.

You've done something like this: inched close to a bank and searched a stream for indications of what the fish are taking. You then see a few caddis come off, but the rises are not the slashing ones you associate with caddis. A few sulphurs ride the currents, but the fish aren't taking these either. The more subtle bulging rises suggest some kind of emerger, a smaller fly being masked by the others. The fish are coming up in good numbers now, and a few dainty flies appear in the fading light of dusk. Pale Evening Duns, you surmise without scooping any in a nymph net. You tie on a #18 soft hackle wet, and the fish takes on the first strike! Problem solved. You take a few more fish, none bigger than thirteen inches, before it is too dark to continue. Your skills have met the test for that evening. You leave the stream feeling content, unable to disguise your sense of fulfillment with your pretensions of stoic indifference. After you've accumulated enough experience, your knowledge base expands and the experience becomes rhythmic and natural as opposed to studied and technical, and that's what makes the sport so fulfilling for many.

My most satisfying fish are the skittish wild brown trout caught on wispy tippets in the slow glides of Pennsylvania's limestone streams. Everything in that equation approaches perfection, the degree of difficulty high. The trout is wild, nervous, and vigorous. It has been fished over many times, and it remembers with vivid, horrid clarity the life-and-death struggles the few other times it has been hooked. Slight movements and shadows remind it of the fisher kings on stilted legs or with clenching talons that have stolen its brothers or cousins from that unsafe underworld. Against many odds, I fool this fish into taking. With the rod bending stoutly, I guide the fish gently away from the elodea as it struggles forcefully against 8x tippet. I keep the hook in its stiff jaw as that trout thrashes forcibly in its last gasp attempt to break free. All the terms I've set for myself and this desperate fish are achieved as I feel it come to my hand. Having accepted the challenge and won, I stare into the fish's anxious eyes before releasing it. I've now made it tougher for someone else to do the same—raised the stakes, upped the ante, defined new terms for the same fish. And you have done the same when you fish the more popular, technical streams near you, the home waters that you've come to cherish.

So what's the appeal of fishing the small streams? There is some measure of difficulty, mostly associated with casting, but the fish are tiny by comparison and they seem to come to the fly with much more ease. There is more of a sense of being near the beginning and end of things at the same time. Another side of ourselves needs exploring, the side that wonders in awe at the aspects of nature that suggest mystery and introspection. The headwaters, where our cherished streams begin, offer a glimpse of the world as a seemingly uncomplicated place where we can intrude for a brief period to explore the workings of nature without interference from the inflictions of our callous society's indifference to nature's grand mysteries. These surroundings convey a feeling of solace, where the fishing becomes unimportant. Instead, our fascination with the place itself causes us to rest on a fallen tree trunk to scan the terrain and reflect on our own circumstances, with the occasional meddling of a romping squirrel or flitting birds to distract us from our thoughts. These places also represent the end of the journey for our precious trout who came up from the sea eons ago, who can go no further. And for ourselves there is a point beyond which we do not venture. The pools thin and become the shallow homes of dace and salamanders, tadpoles, and water skaters. The upstream migration of all the creatures that once inhabited the great oceans of the world dwindles to a handful of fitful forms on the very borders of existence. During drought years these are the places that dry up into little separated pools, pushing the tiny aquatic inhabitants to the edge of life, and at the same time remind us of the margins of our own creation. You can almost see the fear in their faces as you get down on hands and knees and stare in the pools rippling with the nervous flight of these creatures to whatever hiding places are left. I feel comforted that they still have a protective response to impending danger, that they somehow have an instinctive striving to persist, however dire the circumstances. It will ensure their survival. At the same time, I stare at my own reflection after the pool has stilled and feel my own fear were I, an uninvited intruder, to try to survive in this lonely, desolate glen.

I retreat from this timeless place toward the domain where I know best how to survive, my fear and loneliness hidden by my own guileful scheming. On the way back down, I drink in the views before me and get sustenance even when there are no fish to remember. I recall the pleasant intrusions to my solitude on other streams from previous journeys. A mink family crossing the rocks along the banks of the upper Saranac ignored me as I dropped a nymph into a dark, swirling, boulder-strewn pool. A great horned owl stood sentinel one evening on a high oak branch over Pennsylvania's Sherman's Creek while I cast for bass in a bend pool. I was surprised, then pleased, that a river otter disturbed the quiet of the Paper Mill Pool on the Tulpehocken, interrupting me and the trout during an evening caddis hatch late one September. These experiences enhance fishing in a way that is rarely gauged when we use fish caught, size, or challenge as our measures of success.

There isn't any doubt in my mind that we fish to be in pleasing surroundings. Most of us are not employed as guides, park rangers, or naturalists. We spend our time in offices, shops, cars, or airports cutting deals, producing articles of worth, or servicing a complex technology. Trout streams, even our urban trout refuges, and other places where we do our fly-fishing are more comforting places. The features of natural beauty melt our stresses, and the act of fly-fishing absorbs our concentration so completely that the experience is elevated to a plane that conveys our near worship of the sport. Part of what makes these surroundings so pleasant is the detachment that they allow. If our everyday lives are filled with multisensory experiences that have a cumulative effect of burden and strain, then fly-fishing in these wonderful natural reserves gives our lives a sense of balance that nourishes us in ways that are difficult to obtain by other pursuits, an opportunity for reflection that allows an immersion to the inner self.

For a few, I imagine fly-fishing serves as a vehicle for mysticism, a way of transporting oneself to a spiritual realm where intense examination of the self leads to attaining high spiritual understanding. Eugen Herrigel in his *Zen in the Art of Archery* describes his reasons for taking up archery in his pursuit of the understanding of Zen.

"...I became increasingly aware that I could only approach these esoteric writings from the outside; and though I knew how to circle around what one may call the primordial mystic phenomenon, I was unable to leap over the line which surrounded the mystery like a high wall."

His immersion into "artless art" led him to explore the Zen meaning of "detachment," the process of ridding oneself of the ego, or self, in preparation to accept the "transcendent Deity." Fly-fishing can then become a way of immersion into a resplendent consciousness. It means the relinquishing of any purpose of fly-fishing except the act of doing it at the moment. You could find these meditative anglers staring intently across the horizon while seeking the desolation of high mountain streams, casting hookless flies on high-rise roof tops in the middle of an urban center, or sitting on fallen logs with rod across knees, staring silently ahead, oblivious to all surroundings. It's an approach to fishing analogous to the Zen masters who declare, "I eat when hungry, I sleep when tired." For a Zen angler the statement might allow, "I fish when the mood strikes, and I cease when it departs." For these holy souls the path alone rewards.

I've come to regard fishing less-traveled streams as a preferable experience, even if they feature fewer fish. Exploring little rivers without reputation always seems to yield a few surprises if you can accept the premise that grand fish are not a necessary factor for a quality experence. Fishing a moderate-sized stream, say 20 or 30 feet wide, third-or fourth-order tributary, provides me with the same opportunities for solitude and introspection that the smaller tributaries allow, with a couple of significant differences. For one, the stream's larger size permits traditional fly-fishing. That is to say, the casting is unencumbered when compared to the surroundings of tiny tributaries. I'm not suggesting that there are no difficult casts to make, because most streams in the east have some kind of obstacle to overcome from time to time. Casting a fly is the essence of fly-fishing. It is what makes it a significantly different form of fishing than bait-casting or spin-casting. The rhythm of fly-casting feels so wonderful because it is an act unto itself that could well be separated from fishing and still be regarded as whole. The streaming line slicing through the air caused by our artful motions defines a kind of freedom that expresses subtle joy. Because of its larger size, the modest stream is more likely to harbor a stately fish or two, certainly not in the numbers of the more famous or heavily fished ones, but a sixteen-inch brown or a fourteen-inch smallmouth are certainly within the range of possibility. If that stream flows through the natural surroundings that draw us to such places on that power alone, then all the elements are present for treasured moments of indifferent pleasure—the challenge of fighting a large fish with a perfectly matched fly, or the isolation for contemplative moments with nothing else to show for it except for the swaying of a rod to a cadence that declares our fishing passion.

*　　　*　　　*　　　*　　　*　　　*　　　*　　　*

As a trout stream, much of the Manatawny Creek in eastern Berks County is marginal water. It is primarily a stocked, put-and-take affair that has its following diminished by the full creels of its more dedicated factions. There are a few pockets where a wild fish can be found in the main stem, though some of the headwater streams harbor populations of wild browns that are the descendants of stocked refugees that were smart enough to make their way up to the cooler flows. Its lone claim to fame that I could find in the angling literature is a story written by Paul Brown in the 1932 edition of *Field and Stream* titled "Dirty Work at the Covered Bridge." It's a disjointed tale illustrating the belief that a smart old bass can be caught on some kind of bait even when they're not biting, though it may mean discovering that horse-drawn wagons over a covered bridge dislodges ants and grubs into the water below, or that cow flop contains maggots that attract unsuspecting bass. It's not anything like the technical pieces you find in fishing magazines today, instead offering refreshingly homespun wisdoms as outmoded and timeless as covered bridges themselves. Even today the Manatawny is not a bad smallmouth stream if you catch it in the right mood, though I haven't caught the covered bridge hatch yet.

Several years ago, on a cool morning in mid-June, I decided to see if I could track down a few holdover trout that the frying pan adherents may have overlooked in their attempts to clean out the stream. I tucked my van over into one of those pull-outs created when many vehicles persistently park along a likely spot by the stream, this particular one downstream from a bridge pool. After stringing my rod and flapping into my trinket-adorned vest, I made my way down the grassy bank to the edge of the stream. Kneeling down, I wet my fingers, not expecting the water to feel so brisk given the warmth of the preceding few days. My stream thermometer registered a very acceptable 66 degrees, which should have signaled an ideal feeding foray for any lingering trout that might still be in residence. Though I had not fished this stream in several years, nor this particular stretch ever, I was feeling rather assured that this would be a good morning. It's a kind of confident anticipation an angler gets after judging many mornings where the conditions of the day and on the stream seem to indicate a measure of success.

My search of the stream surface for hatches revealed a few tan and green caddis, about size #18, and a couple of blue-winged olives in the range of about #20 to #22. Downstream from my perch, several rise forms appeared in a slow glide next to a sharp riffle, about thirty seconds apart. I crept along the bank, careful not to step into the water until I was closer to my casting position. About thirty feet away from the rises, I sidestepped into the stream, measuring enough room for a backcast to avoid the fresh elderberry shoots leaning into the shallows. A size #18 caddis dry would be my first choice here. Fish seem to slash at caddis more so than mayflies, and I wanted the fish to strike with abandon, so I fastened one to the tippet and prepared to cast. I gazed up through the canopy of oaks and maples to the clean, blue sky then panned like a movie camera across my immediate surroundings. The stubby, brushy willows leaning over the bank on the opposite shore appeared to be reaching out above the water's surface as if poised for some kind of offering to the stream. My fly would land right below these outstretched branches, and with a good mend, I could get a six-foot drift before I would have to lift the line and cast again. I cast and drifted the fly, letting it float passively, only to watch it pass untouched through the glide where the closest rise appeared earlier. A second cast skirted along the same drift line. A sharp swirl marked the instant the fly disappeared, and I pulled the rod back swiftly, trying not to be too forceful. The resistance is light. The sharp zigs and zags signal to me immediately that I've hooked a sunfish. Five inches. Released. An ounce of disappointment fills the back of my mind. In the same glide, there is another rise. Perhaps this time it will be a trout. I'm careful with the cast and there is an immediate take. The weak bend in the rod reveals another sunfish. He puts up a noble fight, though I'm not impressed. In fact, I'm becoming more frustrated, thinking that my valuable fishing time is being wasted on water where there appear to be no trout.

I'm beginning to feel resentful of this place and am psychologically kicking my own ass for not choosing one of a dozen trout streams within a short drive where I could have met a morning hatch with more success. After many more casts, I press on farther downstream. The sun is higher now, too late to move on. The glide turns into a riffle with shallow pockets behind a few boulders. I start to stumble over smaller rocks, realizing that carelessness has overtaken my mental edge. I toss a few more casts in what are becoming fewer and less likely feeding lies. Feeling defeated, I move over to the bank and step up to the solid ground. There is a path before me, slightly off to my right, heading back to the same road where my van is parked. I take a few steps and am surprised by what I've encountered. Suddenly, I'm surrounded on all sides by a large patch of wild black raspberries. The drooping bushes are full of clusters of plump, ripe berries weighting the boughs toward the ground with their succulent fruits. I leaned my rod against a nearby tree and loosened the zipper on my vest. Careful not to prick my waders, I stepped into a small opening in the patch and began plucking handfuls of moist berries off the vines and filling my mouth. After several mouthfuls, I was reminded of the times when I was a young boy taking a short-cut home through a farmer's field after baseball practice. In June, the two old, black cherry trees that were on the border of a cornfield would be fecund with fruit clusters. My friends and I would spend hours perched on the branches of those two trees after practice, gorging on the ripened, sweet black cherries until our lips and tongues were purple and our stomachs distended from our gluttony. We would slowly descend the trees and bend over to pick up our gloves and bats, careful not to put too much pressure on our sated bellies, and waddle home forgetting all about baseball, the harping of the coaches, or the teasing of the more competent players. In this instance, I'd forgotten about fishing; this bountiful clump of berry bushes on the banks of the Manatawny offered a delicious surprise. My nimble fingers plucked a few more berries as I squashed them with my tongue, the sweet nectar of the berries lingering in my mouth. I sidestepped from bush to bush, inspecting nature's gracious offering with a solemn appreciation as I moved to each new stem. The pleasure of this experience began to override my previous feelings about this place and the stream itself. I completed my brief tour through this berry patch, without overindulging. It seems that the paths that lead you to the less-traveled streams offer a kind of wisdom that allows you to recognize your need for balance and boundaries, so I left the rest there as a tithing for the catbirds and jays that frequent these banks or the next fortunate soul who stumbles across this neglected, delightful place. Feeling satisfied, I slowly turned back to get my rod and lazily ambled up the dirt trail toward my van. The question that occurred to me over this short saunter had an immediate and defining reply. Why fish? For the wild black raspberries.

EPILOGUE

In the summer of 2020, I had the fortunate opportunity to seek a bucket-list fish in Montana, the Arctic grayling. Making my way over the pass from the Bitterroot Valley to Wisdom, I was buoyed by a news feature I read in *Trout* magazine about the completion of a fencing project along the upper Big Hole River to protect the habitat of a fish that is barely hanging on the lower forty-eight. When I arrived at my destination river I was greatly disheartened. Yes, there was a ranch with streambank fencing along the river, but it was a very small segment compared to the amount of acreage parallel to the river. Upstream, there were miles upon miles of the Big Hole's upper reaches crowded on both sides of the river with what looked to be thousands of head of beef cattle freely accessing the stream. When I made my way to the river about eight miles downstream of the town, I saw water and river bottom that was full of algae, no doubt choking the oxygen out of the stream and limiting aquatic diversity including those fragile fish. I eventually caught two but returned them immediately without photographing them as any further insult to these fish seemed beyond inappropriate.

Free grazing cattle accessing tributaries is a problem rampant in the western United States. M.R. Montgomery in his 1995 book *Many Rivers to Cross* lamented the loss of indigenous cutthroat trout in several high desert and western landscapes, including his native Montana Since that time, many state wildlife agencies and NGO's have initiated efforts to restore these species to some semblance of sustainable populations. In Chapter 12 "Perkiomen Nightmares," I highlighted the stream restoration activities of Perkiomen Valley Trout Unlimited as primarily engaging in streambank fencing efforts, and while the results after one season are remarkable on their own, the twenty-year lookback with a different lens produces a new set of considerations for me. The farms in that part of Pennsylvania are struggling, with market forces squeezing them mercilessly out of viable business models. It got me to thinking that we may need 'fish-friendly' marketing boosts in the same vein as "wild caught" and "organic" certification and other labeling incentives alerting consumers to purchasing decisions that favor environmentally friendly practices. Pulling something like that off is well beyond my pay grade, and I don't know how complicated the process is, but farmers who do the right thing need to be rewarded and those who don't need to feel a different market force that affects their bottom line in such a way as to hasten them to make necessary changes to their farming practices. I met a few Arctic grayling who would appreciate the effort and I think it is a conversation worth having that could cover a whole range of species, not just coldwater varieties.

In my own life experience, I have embraced the notion of longevity. It's mostly a selfish desire to spend as much time here on the only planet in the known universe to host a magnificent breadth and depth of lifeforms. Fly-fishing allows me to encounter a great array of them and I'd like to do it for as long as I can. While investigating the topic, it turns out that a lot of food science research has been produced in the last twenty years, most of it pointing toward the connection between whole food plant-based diets and prevention of dietary-related diseases. Back in 1978, my acquaintance Blossom, who you met in Chapter 3, was on the right track whether either of us knew it at the time. Our healthcare system and the expenses associated with it are near the point of no longer being sustainable. Most of the costs are attributed to treating the diseases of metabolic syndrome, conditions like type 2 diabetes, heart failure, stroke, obesity, high blood pressure, and high cholesterol to name the most prevalent. Virtually all of these conditions can be prevented or treated by diet. I refer you to Dr. Joel Fuhrman for a starting point if you doubt my assertion. When Dan Buettner, author and investigator of the Blue Zones, started to uncover the world-wide secrets of longevity, the common culinary thread among these far-flung places was a whole food, plant-based diet. These are enclaves of people whose diet consisted largely of unprocessed whole grains, high-carbohydrate nutritious root vegetables (think sweet potatoes), beans and legumes, and green, leafy vegetables. Meat was consumed sparsely, used more as a condiment or flavoring than as a meal portion. For the most part, these societies are considerably less wealthy than the average American family, the exception being the Seventh-day Adventists of Loma Linda, California. Yet they have centenarians among them living at rates far exceeding those in the US, where healthcare is more widely available (but extremely expensive). With that longevity comes a greater vitality, that is, continuing to be a functioning human being instead of being confined to wheelchairs, nursing homes, or hospice care for long periods of senior life. There is a food revolution quietly taking place in this country. Vegan, vegetarian, and flexitarian diets along with the appearance of plant based "mock meats" and meats cloned in manufacturing facilities will likely revolutionize human nutrition. A diet with 90 percent less meat, eaten occasionally or in a mix with soups and stews in far smaller quantities can make enormous contributions to our collective health and that of the planet. I have moved my own diet in that direction with numerous positive results. It is not as hard as it might appear at first glance.

If the Standard American Diet (SAD) evolves to a whole food, plant-based diet, most of our watersheds will have a chance to recover. Realize how many tributaries will be improved and enhanced when they are not grazed over incessantly. Climate science studies indicate that animal agriculture is the seconding leading cause of greenhouse gas emissions after fossil fuels and the leading cause of deforestation, water and air pollution, and loss of biodiversity. Simply put, if the rest of the world ate like Blossom or those folks in the Blue Zones, our collective selves would live longer and healthier lives, have a far less polluted environment, and allow a considerable recovery of our natural world. Ranchers, particularly in the West, would be wise to transition to an eco-tourism economy, where greater population growth will likely spur outdoor recreation to a more enhanced degree than already exists. These transitions will take time but are a future that I would place bets on as having more and greater diversity of fish and wildlife, a climate less stressed, and one in which our children and grandchildren will be able to thrive and enjoy. I know all of the above is a long way from casting for a fine trout in remote regions, but there are actions we need to consider beyond streambank fencing and inadequate culverts to improve our creeks, lakes, and rivers. For many of us, there is a lot of competition for our time and logging volunteer hours for our local streams can become a challenge. However, guiding your home water's most favorable fishing prospects, the planet's best future, and your own optimal health may begin with the contents of your grocery cart. Some food for considerable thought.

ACKNOWLEDGMENTS

First and foremost I would like to thank my wife Carol who supported me throughout this endeavor with encouragement and patience and for taking the time to read many of the drafts included in this book, offering suggestions and valuable insights along the way. This book could never have been completed without her. As my companion in life and sometimes fishing partner, I will always be indebted.

Many thanks to Tor and Daisy for nudging me to change the title of the book and their thoughtful critiques of some of the chapters.

An angler is always immersed in the bounty of nature, and a true outdoors person is one keenly observant of the wild creatures and fascinating plant life surrounding our fishing environs. Thank you Woodstock Girl for introducing me to rufous-sided towhees, black-crowned night herons, dippers, grebes, eastern phoebes, wood anemones, Quaker ladies, cinquefoil, trailing arbutus, and all the other wonderful native species I've come to appreciate while seeking the mysteries of rivers.

My appreciation of wild fish, particularly native fish in their original habitats could not have happened without my friend Chaz, whose passion for the wild and native drove our quest to make the Perkiomen a better place. We've logged many a mile in trucks and in waders taking stream temperatures, talking to landowners, and fishing intently in our quest to restore the Perkiomen.

I am grateful to Lee Hartman, Rick Nyles, and Jerry Kustich for taking the time to read the manuscript and offering back cover endorsement commentary. Their public praise of this volume is immeasurable and received by me with great humility.

My very good friend Bob Myrick, whose generosity is without question, graciously donated the covered bridge pen and ink drawing on the cover.

Tor Steiner and Tom Allen were kind enough to allow me to use their photographs on the back cover.

Hayden Seder thoroughly edited my original manuscript and offered thoughtful suggestions as well as monitoring for conformity to Chicago Manual style.

Lastly, I would like to acknowledge all those who I came in contact while a member of the Perkiomen Valley Chapter of Trout Unlimited including past and present board members, volunteers, cooperating landowners, partners from the Perkiomen Watershed Conservancy, the Delaware Riverkeeper Network, Tulpehocken Chapter of Trout Unlimited, Pine Creek Valley Watershed Association, the Berks County Conservancy (now Berks Nature), the Pennsylvania Fish and Boat Commission, the Pennsylvania Department of Environmental Protection, the Pennsylvania Council of Trout Unlimited and the national Trout Unlimited organization. For fear of leaving someone out by name, you know who you are and I appreciate the effort you give to make streams in our watersheds a better place. I have great optimism for our children's future because of you.